m

Alternatives
to Prisons

Alternatives to Prisons

Other books in the At Issue series:

Alternatives to Prisons

Jennifer Skancke, *Book Editor*

Bruce Glassman, *Vice President*
Bonnie Szumski, *Publisher*
Helen Cothran, *Managing Editor*

GREENHAVEN PRESS
An imprint of Thomson Gale, a part of The Thomson Corporation

Detroit • New York • San Francisco • San Diego • New Haven, Conn.
Waterville, Maine • London • Munich

For more information, contact
Greenhaven Press
27500 Drake Rd.
Farmington Hills, MI 48331-3535
Or you can visit our Internet site at http://www.gale.com

LIBRARY OF CONGRESS CATALOGING-IN-PUBLICATION DATA

Alternatives to prisons / Jennifer Skancke, book editor.
    p. cm. — (At issue)
Includes bibliographical references and index.
ISBN 0-7377-2693-8 (lib. : alk. paper) — ISBN 0-7377-2694-6 (pbk. : alk. paper)
    1. Alternatives to imprisonment—United States. 2. Corrections—Government policy—United States. 3. Criminals—Rehabilitation—United States.
4. Criminals—Mental health services—United States. 5. Criminal behavior—United States—Prevention. I. Skancke, Jennifer. II. At issue (San Diego, Calif.)
HV9304.A647 2005
364.6'0973—dc22   2004053500

Printed in the United States of America

Contents

Introduction

In 2003 there were over 2.1 million people housed in America's federal and state prisons and jails. For the past thirty-one years the prison population has increased annually, with little evidence of slowing down. America's incarceration rate of 715 per 100,000 residents is higher than any other industrialized nation in the world. If current incarceration rates remain the same, 5 percent of people living in the United States can expect to serve time in prison at some point in their lives.

Part of the reason the current prison population is so high is because of several sentencing policies and laws enacted in the eighties and nineties in an attempt to get tough on crime. Some of these changes include mandatory sentencing laws, increased efforts by law enforcement to arrest drug offenders, "truth in sentencing" laws—which mandate that offenders serve at least 85 percent of their sentences—and the "three strikes and you're out" laws.

While imprisonment is the most widely used solution to combat crime, many analysts contend that it is not the most effective response. These critics maintain that America's dependence on incarceration creates a tremendous cost to taxpayers, does little to deter crime, and is not proven to effectively rehabilitate offenders. For instance, according to the Bureau of Justice Statistics, over two-thirds of released prisoners are rearrested and reconvicted within three years of their release. Those critical of incarceration grant that imprisonment is often a necessary means to safeguard the community from the most violent and dangerous criminals, but they argue that it should not be the only option for the many low-level offenders that occupy America's prisons and jails. In order to reduce the incarceration rate, these commentators claim, America needs to make a concerted effort to implement alternatives to imprisonment.

Experts critical of the increasing use of incarceration to address crime often cite an old maxim: If something doesn't work, try something new. During the past couple of decades increasing emphasis has been placed on creating prison alternatives. In fact, there are several alternatives already being used across the country, including drug courts, mental health courts, electronic monitoring, family-based therapies, and restorative justice. These alternatives provide options in lieu of traditional sentencing policies, which many experts criticize. A problem with most current sentencing policies, they claim, is that sentencing guidelines promote a fixed prison sentence for a given crime. These types of sentences do not consider the individual person and the reasons he or she may have committed the crime in the first place. Nor do they consistently offer appropriate rehabilitation to help the offender.

One of the latest sentencing alternatives is called "defense-based sentencing" or "client specific planning." This model employs sentencing consultants or sentencing specialists to help defense attorneys prepare alternative sentencing proposals, which are presented to the judge at the time of the offender's sentencing. Many of these specialists work in public defender offices or in nonprofit agencies that serve public defenders. Specialists can be a valuable resource to defense attorneys who are often bogged down with the intricacies of sentencing guidelines and who often don't have intimate knowledge of alternative programs.

After sentencing consultants are hired, they compile information about the defendant's background and the circumstances surrounding the offense. In order to create the most appropriate sentencing option for the individual, sentencing specialists look at the offender's prior involvement in the criminal justice system, social and family history, employment history, educational background, physical and mental health, financial status, and future prospects. Many of the options include referrals to drug and alcohol treatment programs, mental health services, and community service programs. Herb Hoelter, cofounder and director of the National Center on Institutions and Alternatives, says, "If you're going to take somebody's life for three, four, or five years, you have the obligation to know everything you can about the person, the crime, the circumstances and anything that was going on—and then make a fair decision."

The ultimate goal of these alternatives is to treat and counsel offenders, have them pay back harm done to victims, and minimize the danger to the community. For example, an artist convicted of tax evasion and conspiracy, who previously had no prior convictions, faced a maximum prison sentence of ten years and a $500,000 fine under current sentencing guidelines.

However, a sentencing specialist created an alternative option, which the judge approved: payment of back taxes, a $30,000 fine, two months in a work release program, and eight hundred hours of community service teaching art to disadvantaged children in Harlem schools. According to Hoelter, this type of punishment is appropriate because it "can deprive a defendant of liberty while contributing to the community."

Proponents of prison alternatives point to other benefits of using defense-based sentencing. First, it does not introduce changes to sentencing procedures because the plans are incorporated into the existing court system, and judges still determine the sentence—they just have more options. Second, this method often utilizes existing community resources and thus does not require a significant amount of additional funding for implementation. Third, according to Rittenhouse, a private transformative justice agency used by many Canadian courts, this type of sentencing "fosters respect and responsibility."

Only time will tell if using defense-based sentencing will help reduce America's high rate of incarceration. One thing is for sure: Many criminal justice experts agree that alternatives to imprisonment are necessary to address America's crime problem.

1

Incarceration Does Not Reduce Crime

John Irwin, Vincent Schiraldi, and Jason Ziedenberg

John Irwin is a professor emeritus in the Department of Sociology at San Francisco State University. Vincent Schiraldi is the founder and executive director of the Center on Juvenile Crime and Justice as well as the Justice Policy Institute. Jason Ziedenberg is the senior policy analyst for the Justice Policy Institute.

The imprisonment of over 1 million nonviolent offenders has led to a prison population explosion in the United States. Prisons are overcrowded as a result of the mandatory sentencing laws put into effect in the early 1990s, which have sent a large number of nonviolent first-time drug offenders to prison. However, despite claims that putting more people in prison reduces crime, studies show that there is no correlation between higher incarceration rates and reduced crime. Moreover, the experience of prison often causes harm to inmates, and many respond to their incarceration experience by committing more crimes when released from prison. Mandatory sentencing laws should be repealed so that nonviolent offenders are not incarcerated for lengthy periods of time, and alternatives to prison should be developed.

Over the past two decades, no area of state government expenditures has increased as rapidly as prisons and jails. Justice Department data released on March 15, 1999, show that the number of prisoners in America has more than tripled over the last two decades from 500,000 to 1.8 million, with states

John Irwin, Vincent Schiraldi, and Jason Ziedenberg, "America's One Million Nonviolent Prisoners," *Social Justice*, vol. 27, 2000, pp. 135–47. Copyright © 2000 by *Social Justice*. Reproduced by permission.

like California and Texas experiencing eightfold prison population increases during that time. America's overall prison population now exceeds the combined populations of Alaska, North Dakota, and Wyoming.

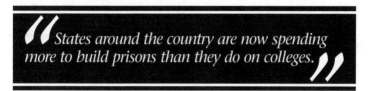

States around the country are now spending more to build prisons than they do on colleges.

What is most disturbing about the prison population explosion is that the people being sent to prison are not the Ted Bundies, Charlie Mansons, and Timothy McVeighs—or even less sensationalized robbers, rapists, and murderers—that the public imagines them to be. Most are defendants who have been found guilty of nonviolent and not particularly serious crimes that do not involve any features that agitate high levels of concern in the minds of the public. Too often, they are imprisoned under harsh mandatory sentencing schemes that were ostensibly aimed at the worst of the worse.

As this analysis will show, the very opposite has been true over the past 20 years. Most of the growth in America's prisons since 1978 is accounted for by nonviolent offenders and 1998 is the first year in which America's prisons and jails incarcerated more than one million nonviolent offenders.

The cost of incarcerating over one million nonviolent offenders is staggering. The growth in prison and jail populations has produced a mushrooming in prison and jail budgets. In 1978, the combined budgets for prisons and jails amounted to five billion dollars. By 1997, that figure had grown to $31 billion. States around the country are now spending more to build prisons than they do on colleges, and the combined prison and jail budgets for 1.2 million nonviolent prisoners exceeded the entire federal welfare budget for 8.5 million poor people last year. . . .

One million nonviolent prisoners

The percentage of violent offenders held in the state prison system has actually declined from 57% in 1978 to 47% in 1997. However, the prison and jail population has tripled over that period, from roughly 500,000 in 1978, to 1.8 million by 1998.

According to data collected by the United States Justice Department, from 1978 to 1996, the number of violent offenders entering our nation's prisons doubled (from 43,733 to 98,672 inmates), the number of nonviolent offenders tripled (from 83,721 to 261,796 inmates), and the number of drug offenders increased sevenfold (from 14,241 to 114,071 inmates). As such, 77% of the growth in intake to America's state and federal prisons between 1978 and 1996 was accounted for by nonviolent offenders.

According to Department of Justice data, 52.7% of state prison inmates, 73.7% of jail inmates, and 87.6% of federal inmates were imprisoned for offenses that involved neither harm, nor the threat of harm, to a victim. Assuming these relative percentages held true for 1998, it can be estimated that by the end of that year, there were 440,088 nonviolent jail inmates, 639,280 nonviolent state prison inmates, and 106,090 nonviolent federal prisoners locked up in America, for a total of 1,185,458 nonviolent prisoners. The combined impact of the growth of prison and jail populations in general—and the accelerated growth of the nonviolent segment of the incarcerated population in particular—has given 1998 the dubious distinction of being the first full year in which more than one million nonviolent prisoners were held in America's jails and prisons for the entire year.

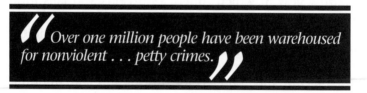

Over one million people have been warehoused for nonviolent . . . petty crimes.

Over one million people have been warehoused for nonviolent, often petty crimes, due to our inability to—or our choice not to—sort out America's lingering social problems from those that threaten us with real harm. The prison system looms so large on our political horizon that it is often difficult for Americans to conceive of its size and scale, or to comprehend how out of kilter it is with the rest of the industrialized world. Consider the following:

- Our nonviolent prison population, alone, is larger than the combined populations of Wyoming and Alaska.
- The European Union, a political entity of 370 million, has a prison population, including violent and nonviolent of-

fenders, of roughly 300,000. This is one-third the number of prisoners that America, a country of 274 million, has chosen to incarcerate just for nonviolent offenses.
- The 1,185,458 nonviolent offenders we currently lock up represents five times the number of people held in India's entire prison system, even though it is a country with roughly four times our population.

As we incarcerated more and more people for nonviolent offenses, African Americans and Latinos comprised a growing percentage of those we chose to imprison. In the 1930s, 75% of the people entering state and federal prison were white (roughly reflecting the demographics of the nation). Today, minority communities represent 70% of all new admissions, and more than half of all Americans behind bars.

At yearend in 1996, there were 193 white American prison inmates per 100,000 whites, 688 Hispanic prison inmates per 100,000 Hispanics, and 1,571 African American prison inmates per 100,000 African Americans. This means that blacks are now imprisoned at eight times the rate of whites and Latinos are imprisoned at three and one-half times the rate of whites. Increasing incarceration rates for African Americans have been driven largely by increases in drug sentencing over the past two decades.

Ironically, women represent both the fastest growing and least violent segment of prison and jail populations. Women made up three percent (12,927) of state prisoners in 1978, a figure that grew to 6.3% (79,624) by 1997. Only 27.6% of male jail inmates are violent offenders, and an even smaller 14.9% of female jail inmates are in for violent offenses. Sixty-four percent of male jail inmates have not been arrested for an act of violence on their current or any prior offense. That is true for 83.1% of female jail inmates.

The financial costs

The cost of incarcerating over one million nonviolent offenders is nothing short of staggering. At a time when our political leaders celebrate the end of big government, prisons, jails, and the services that go into them constitute one of the largest and fastest growing parts of the public sector.
- According to the Criminal Justice Institute, it cost $20,224.65 to incarcerate one jail inmate for one year in 1997. Assuming the costs did not rise between 1997 and

1998, this would mean that the cost of jailing the 440,088 nonviolent jail prisoners was $8.9 billion.

- State inmates cost an average of $19,801.25 to incarcerate per year. That means that, in 1998, it cost $12.7 billion to lock up 639,280 nonviolent state prisoners.
- Federal prisoners cost an average of $23,476.80 per year to imprison. The tab for incarcerating 106,090 nonviolent federal prisoners in 1998 comes to $2.5 billion.
- In 1998, American taxpayers spent a total of $24 billion to incarcerate over one million nonviolent offenders, many of whom had either never been locked up before or who had committed no prior acts of violence.

These figures should be considered conservative because they do not include facility construction costs, which in 1997 amounted to an additional $3.4 billion for the 50 states. Further, according to several estimates, there are hidden costs of operating prisons and jails, such as health care and other contracted services, and debt services on prison bonds that probably drive the average annual cost of imprisonment up closer to $40,000.

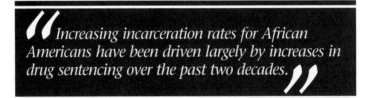

Increasing incarceration rates for African Americans have been driven largely by increases in drug sentencing over the past two decades.

Even without these hidden costs, the amount we spend to incarcerate America's nonviolent offenders is so large that it is difficult to find other government expenditures with which to compare it. The $24 billion figure is almost 50% larger than the entire $16.6 billion the federal government currently spends on a welfare program that serves 8.5 million people. We are spending six times more to incarcerate 1.2 million nonviolent offenders [in 2000] than the federal government will spend on child care for 1.25 million children. While states and counties have lavished money on their prison and jail systems, they have consistently failed to provide adequate funds for educational, health and mental health, and social programs that could have reduced the need for jails and prisons in the first place, thereby feeding the cycle of imprisonment.

One useful way to analyze the scale of prison expenditures is to compare it to what we are currently spending on universities. Prisons and universities generally occupy the portion of a state's budget that is neither mandated by federal requirements, nor driven by population (like K-12 education or Medicare). Because they dominate a state's discretionary funds, prisons and universities must fight it out for the non-mandated portion of the budget.

> *// We are spending six times more to incarcerate 1.2 million nonviolent offenders [in 2000] than the federal government will spend on childcare for 1.25 million children. //*

More important, however, prisons and universities often target the same audience—young adults. As such, the fiscal trade-offs between these two sectors serve as a barometer of sorts, helping to gauge where we are going as a country and what our priorities are. In a series of studies about the shift in funding that has taken place between higher education and corrections, the Justice Policy Institute found:

- States around the country spent more on building prisons than on colleges in 1995 for the first time. That year, there was nearly a dollar-for-dollar trade-off between corrections and higher education, with university construction funds decreasing by $954 million (to $2.5 billion), while corrections funding increased by $926 million (to $2.6 billion). Around the country, from 1987 to 1995, state expenditures for prisons increased by 30%, while expenditures for universities decreased by 19%.
- During the 1990s, the prison budget of New York State grew by $761 million, while its budget for higher education dropped by $615 million.
- From 1984 to 1994, California's prison system realized a 209% increase in funding, compared to a 15% increase in state university funding. California built 21 prisons during that time, and only one state university. There are four times as many African American men in California prisons as in its university system.
- During the 1990s, Maryland's prison budget increased by $147 million, while its university budget decreased by $29 million. Nine out of 10 new inmates added to the

prison system during this period were African American.
- The budget for Florida's corrections department increased by $450 million between 1992 and 1994 alone. That is a greater increase than Florida's university system received in the previous 10 years.
- The District of Columbia literally has more inmates in its prisons than students in its university system.

The dubious crime-control benefits of mass incarceration

Many argue that this growth in imprisonment is a small price to pay for public safety. They say that criminal behavior, no matter how small, must meet with a swift and severe response, lest it grow out of hand. Conservatives such as William Bennett, criminologist John DiIulio, and politicians across the country point to drops in crime over the past five or so years as proof that getting tough on the violent and nonviolent alike has reaped substantial dividends.

There is no doubt that the imprisonment of nearly two million people has prevented some crimes from being committed. Yet as Michael Tonry, a professor of law and public policy at the University of Minnesota, pointed out recently in *The Atlantic Monthly*, you could choose another two million Americans at random and lock them up, and that would reduce the number of crimes too.

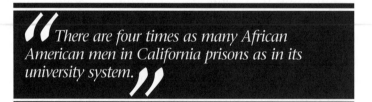

There are four times as many African American men in California prisons as in its university system.

To reasonably conclude that increased incarceration promotes decreases in crime, one would need to show that a jurisdiction with higher growth in its incarceration rate does better from a crime-control standpoint than does a jurisdiction with lower growth in its incarceration rate. If increases in incarceration promote decreases in crime, one would expect that the jurisdictions with the highest growth in imprisonment would do best from a crime-control standpoint. However, in the 10-year period from 1980 to 1991, in which the nation's prison population increased the most, 11 of the 17 states that increased their prison population the least experienced decreases in crime. Of the 13 states that increased their prison populations the most, only seven experienced decreases in crime—a virtual wash. In a previous study, one of the authors [John Irwin] conducted a regression analysis that compared increases in imprisonment with changes in crime in every state in the country and found no relationship between increases in imprisonment and reductions in crime.

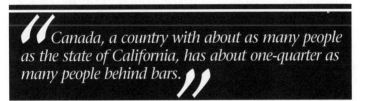

Canada, a country with about as many people as the state of California, has about one-quarter as many people behind bars.

Canada, a country with about as many people as the state of California, has about one-quarter as many people behind bars, and provides a good contrast for judging the crime-control value of mass incarceration. [In 2000], with 4.3 times as many prisoners, California had 4.6 times the homicide rate of Canada. Between 1992 and 1996, Canada increased its prison population by a modest 2,370 inmates (7%), while California's prison population grew by 36,069 inmates (25%). Surprisingly, during that period, homicide rates in Canada and California declined at exactly the same rate of 24% (although, with 2,916 homicide arrests in 1996, California still has five times as many murders as Canada's 581).

[In 2000] the Canadian murder rate has now reached its lowest level since 1969. Thus, for all the billions of dollars California has outspent Canada on keeping people behind bars, Canada is still many times safer than a state of comparable size, and is actually decreasing the rate at which it incarcerates its citizens.

Another way of looking at the effectiveness of mass incarceration is to examine different rates in the United States over time. America's prison population grew at an even greater rate in the five years before the recent drops in crime than it has [since 1995]. So, while there was a 33.6% increase in the incarceration rate from 1987 to 1992, there was a two percent increase in the nation's crime rate, as measured by the FBI Uniform Crime Reports. From 1992 to 1997, there was a 25% increase in the prison population, and a 13% drop in the crime rate. The country actually did better, from a crime-control standpoint, when the prison population grew less precipitously!

The complexities of why crime rates change, and how disconnected they are from the incarceration rate, are best typified by what some call the New York miracle. To be sure, the steady and steep drop in crime in America's largest city is responsible for a sizable portion in the drop in national crime rates. Ironically, New York's crime rate fell even though it has had one of the slowest growing prison systems in the country over the past five years, and the New York City jail system has seen a real decline in the number of people it has held over this period. Between 1992 and 1997, only two states experienced a slower percentage growth in their prison population than did New York—Maryland and Maine. During that period, for example, New York State's prison population grew from 61,736 to 70,026, while its violent crime rate fell by 38.6% and its murder rate by 54.5%.

New York State's modest prison growth provides a solid contrast to the explosive use of incarceration in other states. For example, during that period, California's prison population grew by 30%, or about 270 inmates per week, compared to New York State's more modest 30 inmates per week. By contrast, California's violent crime rate fell by a more modest 23%, and its murder rate fell by 28%. Put another way, New York experienced a percentage drop in homicides that was half again as great as the percentage drop in California's homicide rate, despite the fact that California added nine times as many inmates per week to its prisons than New York did.

> *The damage done to nonviolent offenders by their experience behind bars is at least one reason why the crime-control impact of massive incarceration is disappointing.*

Virtually all of these nonviolent offenders will be released from prison and will try to pick up life on the outside following their profoundly damaging time in prison. For the most part, their chances of pursuing a merely viable, much less satisfying, conventional life after prison are diminished by their time behind bars. The contemporary prison experience often converts them into social misfits and there is a growing likelihood that they will return to crime and other forms of deviance upon release from incarceration. Research by the Rand Corporation confirmed what common sense tells us about the prison experience when it found that convicted felons sent to prison had significantly higher rates of rearrest after release than did similar offenders placed on probation. The damage done to nonviolent offenders by their experience behind bars is at least one reason why the crime-control impact of massive incarceration is disappointing.

Implementing change

The policy implications of imprisoning more than one million nonviolent prisoners are profound and warrant a great deal of public discussion and debate. Over the past two decades, America has rushed headlong into the use of imprisonment as its primary crime-fighting tool. In so doing, small fries have been locked up at far higher rates than have big fish, at enormous social and economic costs, and with little benefit to show for it.

The tide must now be turned and turned abruptly. States and the federal government should abolish mandatory sentencing schemes that send nonviolent offenders to prison for lengthy periods. New York's mandatory sentencing system—dubbed the Rockefeller Drug Laws—cost state taxpayers $680 million in 1998, a figure frighteningly close to the $615 million New York has cut from the annual budget of its university system. A recent analysis by Human Rights Watch concluded that 80% of the nonviolent offenders who received prison sentences in 1997 under the Rockefeller Laws had never been convicted of a violent felony.

Experiments such as those in Minnesota should be replicated nationwide. The change in Minnesota's sentencing law during the 1980s drastically slowed prison growth there and reserved prison space for violent and more serious offenders, while establishing a network of support programs for less serious offenders. Small release valves for dangerously crowded prison systems, like the highly effective use of early release in Illinois, should spread to similarly overcrowded systems around the country. New federal funds (and those now earmarked exclusively for prison construction) should be allocated to help states develop ways to substantially reduce the number of nonviolent prisoners in their systems and to carefully evaluate the impact those reforms have on crime.

We are convinced that little will change unless the debate over crime and punishment can be covered more responsibly by the media. From 1992 to 1996, while homicides throughout the country were declining by 20%, the number of murders reported on the ABC, CBS, and NBC evening news increased by 721%. Six times as many Americans ranked crime as the number one problem in 1996 as in 1992. As long as the public, politicians, and the media focus on the demonic images of Hannibal the Cannibal, our jails and prisons will continue to fill up with the gang that couldn't shoot straight.

At a time [2000] when crime is down, the economy is strong, and no Americans are fighting on foreign soil, we have a unique opportunity to turn our attention to one of our most pressing domestic problems. The cycle of imprisonment has taken on a life of its own, but it is something we created, and as such, something we can change.

2

Incarceration Reduces Crime

Morgan Reynolds

Morgan Reynolds is the director of the Criminal Justice Center at the National Center for Policy Analysis, a nonprofit, nonpartisan think tank. He is also a professor of economics at Texas A&M University.

Crime rates have decreased dramatically as a result of the increased imprisonment of criminal offenders. More stringent sentencing laws and a stronger system of enforcement have helped put offenders behind bars. When the risk of imprisonment increases, crime rates drop. Criminals are fully aware of the consequences of prison and often give up crime so as not to return to prison in the future. Changes in criminal behavior will not come from liberal rehabilitation programs but rather from incapacitation.

Editor's Note: The following viewpoint was originally given as testimony before the U.S. House of Representatives on October 2, 2002.

My name is Morgan Reynolds and I am Director of the Criminal Justice Center at the National Center for Policy Analysis [NCPA], a private, nonprofit, nonpartisan think tank headquartered in Dallas, Texas, and Professor of Economics at Texas A&M University in College Station, Texas. I appreciate the invitation to testify before the [U.S. House of Representatives] subcommittee today [October 2, 2002] on the question of whether or not punishment works to reduce crime.

The answer is obvious to most Americans—yes, of course

Morgan Reynolds, testimony before the House Subcommittee on Crime, Committee on the Judiciary, Washington, DC, October 2, 2002.

punishment reduces crime. Punishment converts criminal activity from a paying proposition to a nonpaying proposition, at least sometimes, and people respond accordingly. We all are aware of how similar incentives work in our lives, for example, choosing whether or not to drive faster than the law allows. (How many of us in this room, for example, have run afoul of law enforcement on a traffic charge?) Incentives matter, including the risks we are willing to run. This is only a commonsense observation about how people choose to behave. Yet controversy over the very existence of a deterrence and incapacitation effect of incarceration has raged in elite circles.

Reduced crime rates

The first duty of a scientist, it's been said, is to point out the obvious. The logic of deterrence is pretty obvious, but I must point to evidence too, which is overwhelming, for the negative impact of punishment on crime. Evidence ranges from simple facts to sophisticated statistical and econometric studies.

Even experts who disagree with each other about some aspects of criminal justice in agreement about deterrence. For example, when *Forbes* magazine asked John Lott, senior research scholar at Yale Law School and author of *More Guns, Less Crime*, "Why the recent drop in crime?" he responded, "Lots of reasons—increases in arrest rates, conviction rates, prison sentence lengths." And Daniel Nagin, a Carnegie-Mellon University professor of public policy who co-authored an article in the *Journal of Legal Studies* critical of Lott's work on concealed carry laws, says in *The Handbook of Crime and Punishment*, Oxford, 1998, "The combined deterrent and incapacitation effect generated by the collective actions of the police, courts, and prison system is very large."

> **//** *'The combined deterrent and incapacitation effect generated by the collective actions of the police, courts, and prison system is very large.'* **//**

In sharp contrast to the situation ten years ago, experts who assert the contrary are fighting a rearguard action. Crime rates have fallen 30 percent over the last decade while the prison and jail population doubled to two million. Most people are able to connect these dots (*The New York Times* aside), and even the academy has caught on. As German philosopher Arthur Schopenhauer said, truth passes through three stages, first, it is ridiculed, second, it is violently opposed, and third, it is accepted as being self-evident.

Simple, everyday facts about crime are easy to explain from an incentive-based perspective and hard to explain from any other perspective:

- The cops are never around when you need them (because criminals are not stupid enough to commit crimes in front of the cops).
- When the police participate in a labor strike or "sick out," crime sprees break out (and in the aftermath of natural disasters, looting runs riot unless the Guard is called up).
- Prison and jail officials daily manage two million less-than-model citizens living in close quarters with few incidents (order is sustained because inmates heed incentives).

Prisons protect society

Given the avarice of man, the hard reality is that the threat of bad consequences, including public retribution posed by the legal system, is vital to secure human rights to life and property against predation. If men were angels, as James Madison said, we'd have no need of government.

The sad part about prisons is that the most effective crime reducer is the intact family. But government policies have gone far to undermine the family, intensifying the crime problem (welfare, taxes, no-fault divorce, etc.). As internal restraints (character, morality, virtue) degrade, we lamentably rely on external restraints to protect civilization, at least in the short run. As Edmund Burke, English political philosopher, said, "Society cannot exist unless a controlling power upon will and appetite be placed somewhere, and the less of it there is within, the more there must be without . . . men of intemperate minds cannot be free. Their passions forge their fetters."

Human behavior

Criminality is purposeful human behavior. The testimony of criminals provides perhaps our strongest evidence that, in the vast majority of cases, lawbreakers reason and act like other human beings (also a fundamental proposition in the justice system). Criminologists Richard Wright and Scott Decker interviewed 105 active, nonincarcerated residential burglars in St. Louis, Mo. Burglar No. 013 said, "After my eight years for robbery, I told myself then I'll never do another robbery because I was locked up with so many guys that was doin' 25 to 30 years for robbery and I think that's what made me stick to burglaries, because I had learned that a crime committed with a weapon will get you a lot of time."

Burglars also choose their targets by considering both risks and rewards. For example:

- Burglars avoid neighborhoods that are heavily patrolled or aggressively policed: "You got to stay away from where the police ride real tough."
- Nine out of 10 burglars say they always avoid breaking into an occupied residence: "I rather for the police to catch me vs. a person catching me breaking in their house because the person will kill you. Sometimes the police will tell you, 'You lucky we came before they did.'"
- Realistically enough, burglars perceive the chance of being apprehended for a given break-in as extremely slim, partly because they efficiently search the master bedroom first (cash, jewelry, guns) and do not linger inside the target.

The value of punishment in crime prevention

Only after World War II did scholars begin to statistically study the effects of deterrence. Today a large body of scholarly literature generally confirms the value of punishment in the prevention of crime.

Perhaps the most widely cited is Isaac Erhlich's 1973 study of punishment and deterrence in the *Journal of Political Economy.* Using state data for 1940, 1950 and 1960, Ehrlich found that crime varied inversely with the probability of prison and the average time served.

More recently, University of Chicago economist Steven Levitt estimated that for each 10 percent rise in a state's prison population, robberies fall 7 percent, assault and burglary shrink 4 percent each, auto theft and larceny decline 3 percent each, rape falls 2½ percent and murder drops 1½ percent. On average, 10 to 15 nondrug felonies are eliminated for each additional prisoner locked up, saving social costs estimated at $53,900, well in excess of the $30,000 it costs annually to incarcerate a prisoner.

Scholars also ask which provides the greater deterrent, certainty or severity of punishment? One provocative study involving prisoners and college students came down firmly on the side of certainty. When tested, both groups responded in virtually identical terms. Prisoners could identify their financial self-interest in an experimental setting as well as students could. However, in their decision making, prisoners were much more sensitive to changes in certainty than in severity of punishment. In terms of real-world application, the authors of the study speculate that long prison terms are likely to be more impressive to lawmakers than lawbreakers.

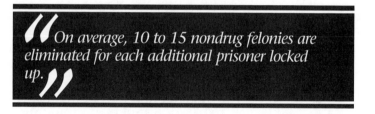

On average, 10 to 15 nondrug felonies are eliminated for each additional prisoner locked up.

Supporting evidence for this viewpoint comes from a National Academy of Sciences panel which claimed that a 50 percent increase in the probability of incarceration prevents about twice as much violent crime as a 50 percent increase in the average term of incarceration.

Nonetheless, severity of punishment also remains crucial for deterrence. "A prompt and certain slap on the wrist," criminologist Ernest van den Haag wrote, "helps little." Or, as Milwaukee Judge Ralph Adam Fine wrote, "We keep our hands out of a flame because it hurt the very first time (not the second, fifth or 10th time) we touched the fire."

Imprisonment reduces crime

Distinguishing between the deterrent and incapacitation effects of prison is empirically difficult, but economists Daniel Kessler and Levitt cleverly separate the two using California data on sentence enhancements. Proposition 8, which imposed longer sentences for a selected group of crimes, reduced these crimes by 4 percent within one year of passage and by 8 percent within three years after passage. These immediate effects are consistent with deterrence since there is no additional incapacitation impact in the short run.

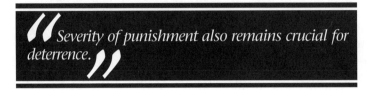

Severity of punishment also remains crucial for deterrence.

If the United States, with so many people in prison, has one of the world's highest crime rates, doesn't this imply that prison does not work? Scholar Charles Murray has examined this question and concluded that the answer is no. Instead, the nation has had to imprison more people in recent years because it failed to do so earlier (the war on drugs also plays a role). Murray compared the record of the risk of imprisonment in England to that in the United States.

- In England the risk of going to prison for committing a crime fell by about 80 percent over a period of 40 years and the English crime rate gradually rose.
- By contrast, the risk of going to prison in the U.S. fell by 64 percent in just 10 years starting in 1961 and the U.S. crime rate shot up.

In the United States, it was not a matter of crimes increasing so fast that the rate of imprisonment could not keep up. Rather, the rate of imprisonment fell first by deliberate policy decisions. By the time the U.S. began incarcerating more criminals in the mid-1970s, huge increases were required to bring the risk of imprisonment up to the crime rate. It is more difficult to reestablish a high rate of imprisonment after the crime rate has escalated than to maintain a high risk of imprisonment from the outset, Murray concluded. We've experienced the same phenomenon in Texas, where crime rocketed up in the 1980s while punishment plunged.

However, both the U.S. and Texas experiences showed that it is possible for imprisonment to stop a rising crime rate and then gradually begin to push it down. The American crime rate peaked in 1980, a few years after the risk of imprisonment reached its nadir. Since then, as the risk of imprisonment has increased, with few exceptions the rates of serious crimes have retreated in fits and starts to levels of 20 or more years ago. My own research for the NCPA (www.ncpa.org) shows that expected punishment has had an inverse correlation with crime rates for both Texas and the nation.

Prevention versus detention in juvenile crime

Juvenile offenders, due to their youth and immaturity, pose a special challenge to the criminal justice system. In the past, many judges and social workers have argued for less stringent treatment of such offenders, with "prevention" taking precedence over detention. The focus tends to be on so-called root causes, rehabilitation and nonpunitive approaches. Yet there is a close connection between lack of punishment and the forming of criminal habits. Recent studies note the effectiveness of punishment for juveniles, not just adults. Between 1980 and 1993 juvenile crime rose alarmingly, and as the states toughened their approach during the 1990s, it declined just as steeply.

Likewise, in his study of criminal justice in England, Charles Murray found that in 1954 the system operated on the assumption that the best way to keep crime down was to intervene early and sternly. Crime was very low, and the number of youths picked up by the police went down by about half as children matured from their early to their late teens. [In 2000], however, a widespread assumption in England (as in the United States) is that youthful offenders need patience more than punishment. England's traditionally low crime rate is now very high, and the number of youths picked up by the police roughly triples from the early to the late teens.

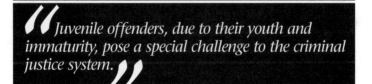

Juvenile offenders, due to their youth and immaturity, pose a special challenge to the criminal justice system.

The need to hold the individual juvenile criminal responsible for his actions does not make incarceration the sole option. For example, Anne L. Schneider found in six random-assignment experiments involving 876 adjudicated (convicted) delinquents in six American cities that victim restitution and incarceration both lowered reoffending while probation did not. Victim restitution meant monetary restitution, community service or work to repay the victims.

The criminal personality

Believers in rehabilitation regard punishment as primitive or counterproductive. For example, Alvin Bronstein, former executive director of the American Civil Liberties Union's National Prison Project, contended that releasing half the nation's prisoners would have little or no effect on the U.S. crime rate.

A major obstacle for such sunny optimism is the existence of what might be called the criminal personality. Perhaps the most important work on this subject is the three-volume study by the late Samuel Yochelson, a physician, and Stanton Samenow, a practicing psychologist. After interviewing hundreds of criminals and their relatives and acquaintances, the two researchers concluded that criminals (1) have control over what they do, freely choosing evil over good, (2) have distinct personalities, described in detail as deceitful, egotistical, myopic and violent and (3) make specific errors in thinking (52 such errors are identified).

> *Believers in rehabilitation regard punishment as primitive or counterproductive.*

Yochelson and Samenow assert that the criminal must resolve to change and accept responsibility for his own behavior. Hardened criminals can reform themselves, but Samenow estimates that only 10 percent would choose to do so. He avoids the word "rehabilitation" when describing chronic criminals: "When you think of how these people react, how their patterns go back to age 3 or 4, there isn't anything to rehabilitate."

Careful studies of well-intended but soft-headed programs continue to find little payoff. In the case of street gang crime, Professor Malcolm Klein found that typical liberal-based gang interventions have failed to manifest much utility. They appeal to our best instincts, but are too indirect, too narrow or else produce boomerang effects by producing increased gang cohesiveness.

Deterrence works

The truth is that changing criminal behavior by means other than deterrence is always problematical. A comprehensive scientific evaluation of hundreds of previous studies and prevention programs funded by the Justice Department found that "some programs work, some don't, and some may even increase crime." The report was prepared by the University of Maryland's Department of Criminology and Criminal Justice for the Justice Department and mandated by Congress. Still, too little is known and the report calls for 10 percent of all federal funding for these programs to be spent on independent evaluations of the impact of prevention programs.

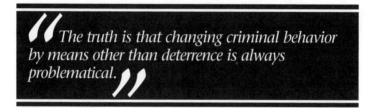

The truth is that changing criminal behavior by means other than deterrence is always problematical.

Public opinion strongly supports the increased use of prisons to give criminals their just desserts. The endorsement of punishment is relatively uniform across social groups. More than three-quarters of the public see punishment as the primary justification for sentencing. More than 70 percent believe that incapacitation is the only sure way to prevent future crimes, and more than three-quarters believe that the courts are too easy on criminals. Three-quarters favor the death penalty for murder.

Still, the public holds out some hope for rehabilitation, too. About 60 percent express hope that services like psychological counseling, training and education inside prison will correct personal shortcomings. Such sentiments are more likely to be expressed on behalf of young offenders than adults, and by nonwhite respondents.

Despite continuing calls for a "better way," what criminals need most is evidence that their crimes do not pay. Neither criminals nor the rest of us "drive a car 100 miles an hour toward a brick wall, because we know what the consequences will be," as author Robert Bidinotto puts it. Punishment flat works. It's unpleasant and expensive, yes, but among other virtues, it supplies the convict with a major incentive to reform. Even career criminals often give up crime because they don't want to go back to prison. The old prescription that punishment be swift, certain and severe is affirmed by modern social science.

As expected punishment plunged during the 1960s and 1970s, crime rose astronomically. When expected punishment began rising in the 1980s and 1990s, crime leveled off and began falling. With the well-publicized success of no-nonsense police tactics like those in New York City, few observers today doubt that the criminal justice system can have a major impact on crime. Does that mean that everything has been done perfectly over the last decade? No, there is plenty of room for improvement in the future, but that is another subject.

3

Punitive Approaches to Addressing Juvenile Crime Are Ineffective

Richard A. Mendel

Richard A. Mendel is a writer, researcher, and consultant on poverty-related issues in youth development, neighborhood safety, employment and training, and community economic development. He has written several articles for the American Youth Policy Forum, a nonprofit, nonpartisan organization that provides policy makers with information about youth policy issues.

Current juvenile justice laws and policies, such as sending juveniles to adult courts and doling out strict punishments, are ineffective in reducing adolescent crime. America's embrace of the idea of "adult time for adult crime" has led to many youths being exposed to dangerous risks in prisons and has not helped deter juveniles from committing crime in the future. The juvenile justice system needs to implement several proven alternatives to prison, such as community-based programs that emphasize the family, in order to reduce adolescent crime and youth violence. However, exaggerated fears about violent youth have kept many states from implementing these successful and cost-effective strategies.

America has both the knowledge and the money we need to substantially reduce adolescent crime and youth violence. We have the know-how to reduce the number of young people likely to join the next generation of adult criminals. Better yet,

Richard A. Mendel, "Less Hype, More Help: Reducing Juvenile Crime, What Works—and What Doesn't," www.aypf.org, 2000. Copyright © 2000 by the American Youth Policy Forum. Reproduced by permission.

we can likely achieve this goal at a cost no greater (and perhaps considerably less) than what we will spend if current juvenile justice policies and programs remain in place.

That's the good news. The bad news is that—at all levels of government—the changes necessary to win the battle against juvenile crime are not being enacted. Even worse, many local, state and federal leaders have instead been passing laws and funding programs that simply don't work—including some very expensive efforts that may actually increase juvenile crime.

These so-called "reforms" have been implemented with strong public support—propelled by a barrage of sensational-ized news coverage in recent years spotlighting heinous crimes committed by young people. Juvenile crime has become front-page news. Public opinion polls have found ever-increasing support for harsher punishment of juvenile offenders. Political leaders across the nation have responded in lock step.

> *Do these approaches to juvenile crime work? Do they produce . . . lower rates of delinquency, reduced recidivism among youthful offenders—and at a reasonable cost?*

Virtually every state in the nation enacted legislation in the 1990s either mandating the transfer of youthful offenders to adult courts or easing the legal process for prosecutors and judges to do so. Most states have also increased punishments for juvenile offenders and/or included juvenile convictions in adult "three strikes and you're out" laws. Most have scaled back privacy protections that historically shielded the identities of juvenile offenders, and most states and cities have significantly expanded the bed capacity of their juvenile detention centers and locked correctional facilities. The federal government has jumped in as well—requiring states to consider new laws to try more youths in adult court as a condition for receiving federal delinquency prevention and juvenile justice funding.

These changes have been made with hardly a whisper of public opposition. As criminologist Peter Greenwood of the RAND Corporation has written, "In recent years it has become fashionable for just about every candidate for public office to have a position on crime, and the only position worth having is appearing to be tougher than your opponent."

But do these approaches to juvenile crime work? Do they produce the results we want—lower rates of delinquency, reduced recidivism among youthful offenders—and at a reasonable cost? Do research and experience demonstrate that these are the most successful and cost-effective approaches to combatting adolescent crime? Or have other less-utilized policies and programs proven more effective? Addressing these questions is essential for any successful response to adolescent crime. Yet such questions have been seldom asked in the stampede to "get tough" with delinquent children and youth. . . .

Winning strategies

Over the past two decades, prevention and juvenile justice policy innovators have developed and validated a number of intervention models that substantially lower either recidivism by youthful offenders or the onset of delinquent behavior by youth at risk for delinquency.

For youth who do not pose an immediate threat to public safety, most of the winning strategies work with young people in their own homes and communities, rather than in institutions, and they focus heavily on the family environment. One strategy, called Multisystemic Therapy, has cut recidivism rates of chronic juvenile offenders by 25 to 70 percent in a series of rigorous clinical trials—and MST costs only $4,500 per youth, less than one-fourth the cost of an eight-month stay in juvenile corrections. Another home-based strategy, Functional Family Therapy, has also reduced the recidivism rates of delinquent youth by 25 to 80 percent in repeated trials. It costs only $2,000 per youth.

> *Most of the winning strategies work with young people in their own homes and communities, rather than in institutions.*

Researchers have also produced valuable information on the causes, correlates and developmental pathways leading to delinquency, and they have identified a solid set of core principles to guide effective prevention practice. Meanwhile, juvenile justice reformers have demonstrated many best practices that markedly improve the success of youth in juvenile courts and corrections systems while saving a significant percentage of taxpayer funds now spent on juvenile justice. The experts still have a world of work to do in honing and refining their instruments, but the basic tools are now available to substantially improve our nation's juvenile justice and delinquency prevention systems.

Exaggerated fears

Alarmist rhetoric about a new generation of juvenile "superpredators" and a "ticking time bomb" of juvenile crime pervaded the public consciousness during the 1990s and diverted political leaders' attention from the crucial task of investing in what works. This rhetoric was unfounded.

After a sharp upswing during the late 1980s and early 1990s, juvenile crime and violence have fallen sharply. By 1998, the latest year for which data are now available, the juvenile homicide rate had declined by 52 percent from its 1993 high—bringing the rate to its lowest level since 1987. The combined rates for all serious violent offenses (murder, rape, robbery, and aggravated assault) declined 32 percent from 1994–98 for youth ages 15–17 and 27 percent for children 14 and under.

Youth remains a period of heightened offending. Both arrest data and self-report surveys show that age 18 is the peak year in life for offending, and that adolescents commit crimes at far higher rates than any group except young adults. The combination of projected growth in the number of adolescents over the next decade and the toxic social conditions that exist today for many children place us in danger of a renewed rise in adolescent crime early in the new century. But exaggerated fears and overheated rhetoric will only distract policymakers and citizens from the critical challenge of erecting the better delinquency prevention and juvenile justice systems we need.

Adult courts are inappropriate for juveniles

Instead of new investments in research and development and broad implementation of proven program models and best practice reforms, political action against youth crime was dominated in the 1990s by new laws to transfer whole classes of adolescent offenders to adult courts and adult corrections. This is the wrong answer to juvenile crime—and should be abandoned at all levels of government.

Far from reducing crime, experience shows that transfer to criminal (i.e., adult) courts actually increases the future criminality of youthful offenders. In study after study, juvenile offenders who are transferred to criminal court recidivate more often, more quickly, and with more serious offenses than those who are retained under juvenile jurisdiction. In Minnesota, 58 percent of transferred youth committed an additional crime within two years versus 42 percent of youth retained in juvenile courts. A Florida study of more than 5,000 offenders found that transferred youth had a higher re-arrest rate (30 vs. 19 percent) and shorter time period to re-arrest (135 days vs. 227 days) than youth retained in the juvenile justice system. Studies in Pennsylvania and New York report similar findings, and other research proves that the threat of being tried as an adult does not deter youth from crime.

> *The basic tools are now available to substantially improve our nation's juvenile justice and delinquency prevention systems.*

Meanwhile, transfer can expose youth to grave risks. Compared with youth confined in the juvenile justice system, juvenile offenders housed in adult jails and prisons are eight times more likely to commit suicide, five times more likely to be sexually assaulted, twice as likely to be beaten by staff, and 50 percent more likely to be attacked with a weapon. Prisons are, however, a great place for youth to learn the tools of the crime trade from grizzled veterans. Moreover, transfers to criminal court severely damage the life chances of youth by staining them for life with a criminal record. Transfers are especially damaging for minority youth—who make up 77 percent of all youth confined in adult prisons. "Adult time for adult crime" is a catchy phrase, but irresponsible public policy.

Juvenile justice is ineffective

Our nation's juvenile justice institutions themselves present significant barriers to implementing effective practices that prevent and reverse delinquent behavior. Though a separate, rehabilitation-oriented system of justice remains the only sensible approach for addressing adolescent crime, the operation of juvenile justice is highly problematic in most states and cities.

Despite stirrings of positive change in some states and localities, most juvenile justice systems continue to devote the great bulk of their resources to confinement of youthful offenders—including many who pose no danger to the community. A 1993 study of 28 states found that only 14 percent of offenders confined in juvenile correctional institutions were committed for serious violent crimes. More than half of the youth in state institutions were committed for property or drug crimes and were serving their first terms in a state institution. Moreover, despite a cost of $100 to $150 per youth per day, delinquents sentenced to youth correctional facilities typically suffer recidivism rates of 50 to 70 percent. A follow-up study on youth released from Minnesota's two correctional "training schools" in 1991 found that 91 percent had been arrested within five years of release. In Maryland, a study of 947 youths released from correctional facilities in 1994 found that 82 percent were referred to juvenile or criminal courts within two and one-half years after release.

Meanwhile, most jurisdictions spend little for home-based, family-oriented, and multi-dimensional rehabilitation strategies that have proven more successful than incarceration in reducing delinquent behavior. Most jurisdictions provide few meaningful responses to the early delinquency of young adolescents, even those at high risk to become chronic offenders. Many pay little attention to results and instead continue to fund many ineffective or counterproductive approaches, rather than replicating methodologies that have been scientifically proven to reduce offending. Meanwhile, unequal treatment of minority youth is pervasive in juvenile justice nationwide, and other violations of adolescents' civil and human rights occur in a disturbing number of states and localities.

Prevention strategies

A new and improved juvenile justice system is necessary but not sufficient to win the battle against juvenile crime. Rather, juvenile justice must be combined with complementary efforts to prevent delinquency before it starts.

Prevention experts have developed an impressive array of

strategies in recent years to preclude the onset of delinquent behaviors and to correct the behavior of pre-adolescent children who display serious conduct problems. Many of the most successful strategies engage parents and improve the home environment of high-risk children. For instance, such early childhood programs as home visits from nurses and enriched pre-school programs for high-rise toddlers have lowered subsequent delinquency by up to 80 percent. Likewise, research-based programs for young children with conduct disorders— providing parenting training for the parents and/or social competency for the children themselves—substantially reduce behavior problems in 70 to 90 percent of cases. Several school-based and community-based prevention strategies have also demonstrated power to reduce delinquent behavior.

> *Exaggerated fears and overheated rhetoric will only distract policymakers and citizens from the critical challenge of erecting the better delinquency prevention and juvenile justice systems we need.*

Unfortunately, many efforts to prevent delinquency suffer from the same weak focus on results that plagues juvenile justice. For instance, a 1997 study of school-based prevention programming in 19 school districts found that "Districts rarely implemented approaches that, according to current research, have the greatest potential for making a difference for students." Failure to implement proven strategies leads communities to squander many opportunities to avert delinquent careers through targeted early childhood programs, research-driven school-based prevention efforts, community-based youth development, and effective mental health treatment for disturbed children at heightened risk for delinquency.

Meeting the youth crime challenge

Thanks to the unprecedented spree of youth violence in the late 1980s and early '90s, overheated rhetoric about juvenile "super-predators" since the mid-1990s, and horrific school shooting tragedies in Columbine and other communities since 1997, adolescent crime and violence have risen to the top of our nation's policy agenda.

Thanks to our growing understanding about the roots of criminality and our increasing arsenal of effective strategies, America has an opportunity to further reduce juvenile crime and hold it down in the years to come. We know how to improve the success of juvenile justice systems in lowering recidivism among delinquent youth, and we know how to avert the onset of delinquent careers through targeted prevention. Many effective solutions cost far less to implement than current policies and programs.

To capture the opportunities for reform, however, states and communities will have to overcome deep-rooted obstacles. Many state and local policymakers lack information about effective practices. Many agencies have limited capacity to plan and develop new programs effectively, and many lack start-up funding to support the spread of promising practices. Meanwhile, the political environment surrounding youth crime issues remains highly charged—exacerbating the tendency of public leaders to avoid risks and shun the kind of wrenching operational changes that would be required of professionals and agencies to implement many reforms. For understandable reasons, then, the deck is now stacked against reforms urgently needed to hold down youth crime rates in the years to come.

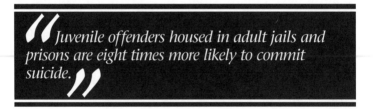

Juvenile offenders housed in adult jails and prisons are eight times more likely to commit suicide.

What will it take to overcome these obstacles and begin building positive momentum for progress against adolescent crime? While the process will be long and complex, the first step is straightforward: We must elevate the debate over youth crime by rejecting the simplistic formulation of "adult time for adult crime" and dismissing proposals to disband juvenile courts or further erode their jurisdiction. Overwhelming evidence proves that transferring youth to adult courts exacerbates the criminality of those transferred and fails to deter crime among other youth. Powerful analysis demonstrates that measured punishments, high-quality treatment services, community-based youth development programming, and freedom from a criminal record are far more effective at turning delinquent youth away from crime than criminal prosecution or incarceration with adult convicts.

Hundreds of years after the introduction of Common Law, the United States led the world in 1899 by creating the first court system in history specifically for young people. Today, separate juvenile justice systems operate in virtually every civilized nation on earth. With public concern over youth crime now atop the list of public concerns, America should not abandon this home-grown solution. Rather, we must re-embrace the juvenile justice ideal and dedicate ourselves to retooling and reforming our juvenile justice and delinquency prevention systems to meet the demands of a new century.

Reshaping juvenile justice

Herein lies the more difficult challenge: strengthening and reshaping juvenile justice and delinquency prevention efforts nationwide to capitalize on our rapidly increasing knowledge of what works. Specifically, five areas of strategic action offer the greatest promise:

1. End Over-Reliance on Corrections and Other Out-of-Home Placements for Delinquent Youth. In most states, local juvenile courts face a strong financial incentive to commit troubled youth to state correctional institutions rather than treat them locally—even for youth who pose no threat to public safety. Likewise, most of the costs for placing troubled youth into group homes and residential treatment centers are reimbursed typically with federal, state, or private insurance funds. By contrast, the costs to retain youth at home and provide community-based supervision and treatment are paid entirely by the locality in most states. To reverse this counterproductive dynamic, states should revise their funding formulas to reward localities for serving youth in their homes and communities whenever possible and also require localities to pay a share of the costs when they commit non-dangerous youth to state correctional facilities. Likewise, states should reduce unnecessary placements of delinquents and otherwise-troubled youth to group homes and residential treatment centers by developing "systems of care" reforms that reward child welfare agencies and other service providers for minimizing over-reliance on out-of-home placements.

2. Invest in Research-Based Interventions for Juvenile Offenders, as well as Research-Based Prevention. The advances produced by delinquency scholars and researchers over the past two decades can revolutionize America's approach to juvenile crime. In fact, the new evidence demands drastic change, because it demonstrates clearly that today's common practices are often ineffective, even counterproductive. Based on these findings, the federal government and foundations should invest heavily in the replication and further refinement of effective strategies and in continuing research efforts to develop even better strategies for quelling delinquent conduct among troubled youth. Juvenile justice agencies at all levels should invest in the widespread implementation of promising and proven strategies, and they should eliminate or modify strategies that don't work.

3. Measure Results, Fund What Works, and Cut Funds to What Doesn't Work. Substantive information about programs, services, budgets and especially outcomes is hard to come by in most juvenile justice agencies. This scarcity of hard facts presents both a critical problem today and an opportunity to spur meaningful reforms in the future. As noted above, the available evidence shows that many current juvenile justice and delinquency prevention efforts are not effective. Thus, measuring results is critical. The federal government should make concrete, standardized evaluation a requirement for all states and localities receiving federal juvenile justice and delinquency prevention funds. Given the federal government's central role in research and development, and given its small percentage of the nation's overall juvenile justice and delinquency prevention budgets, developing new knowledge must be a core goal for all federal spending. State and local leadership is also critical for data collection and program evaluation. Juvenile justice agencies nationwide should create outcome databases to measure the effectiveness of all juvenile justice programs. These data will allow policymakers and the public to clearly identify what is working and what isn't. This information is critical to build momentum for substantive reform of youth crime reduction efforts.

4. Engage Community Partners. Two of the characteristic traits of youth who fall into delinquent lifestyles are lack of attachment to caring adults and lack of involvement in school and other positive, pro-social activities in their communities—an after-school program, a job, church, community service. "Disconnected" youth comprise the lion's share of the delinquency population. In many localities, juvenile courts and juvenile justice agencies also suffer from a "disconnection" problem. While they routinely refer youth to service providers in their communities, many juvenile courts have not formed strong working partnerships with partner agencies, community organizations, or local citizens to help fill in the missing pieces in delinquent youths' lives. States should encourage or even require juvenile courts and probation agencies to strengthen partnerships with residents, community-based organizations, and partner agencies. At the local level, juvenile justice leaders must re-connect youth to caring adults and positive activities in their communities through innovative "restorative justice" initiatives such as family-group conferences, community accountability boards, teen courts, drug courts, and Youth Aid Panels; and they should establish multi-agency teams to jointly assess and oversee treatment of high-risk youth involved in the child welfare, education, juvenile justice, and mental health systems.

5. *Mobilize Whole Communities to Study, Plan and Implement Comprehensive Strategies for Combatting Youth Crime.* Since 1994, the Office of Juvenile Justice and Delinquency Prevention has provided funds for more than 600 communities to undertake comprehensive planning for new and improved efforts to prevent delinquency and related problem behaviors (such as substance abuse, teen pregnancy, and school failure), and to strengthen local responses when youth do commit crimes. Despite positive results, some proposals are now pending in Congress to eliminate this federal funding stream. Congress should reject these proposals and instead continue and expand funding for comprehensive community analysis, planning, and mobilization. With or without federal support, states should emulate the example of states like Kansas, North Carolina, Pennsylvania, and Texas by requiring local jurisdictions to create local policy boards and develop comprehensive community plans. Likewise, localities on their own should mobilize public officials, community leaders and residents to undertake intensive analysis, planning, and program development.

Americans are right to view youth crime as a major concern for our society. If we are willing to roll up our sleeves and get to work, effective solutions are now available. The time has come for communities and political leaders to rise to this challenge.

4

Prison Overcrowding Creates a Need for Prison Alternatives

Alida V. Merlo and Peter J. Benekos

Alida V. Merlo is associate professor of criminology at Indiana University of Pennsylvania. Peter J. Benekos is professor of criminal justice at Mercyhurst College in Erie, Pennsylvania. Merlos and Benekos are coeditors of Corrections: Dilemmas and Directions.

America's prevalent crime control strategy—incarceration—has created an exploding prison population. The emphasis on incarceration stems from "get tough on crime" policies, the media's sensationalism of crime, new minimum sentencing laws, and the war on drugs. However, punitive crime control policies do little to rehabilitate prisoners or prevent recidivism. Moreover, the construction and management of prisons creates substantial financial costs to society. Alternatives to prisons such as intensive probation, house arrest, and electronic monitoring, should be implemented to reduce new prison construction and the financial burden of incarceration.

After seven years of decreasing rates of violent crime, incarceration is still viewed as a salient crime control strategy for dealing with crime and criminals. Beginning in 1790 with the Walnut Street Jail in Pennsylvania, policy makers have consistently demonstrated enthusiasm for expanding, renovating, and relying on jails and prisons to deal with offenders. In fact, in recent years the United States has demonstrated an even greater commitment to constructing prisons and increasing the nation's inmate population. . . .

Some of the factors which account for the emphasis on incarceration include the media sensationalism of crime, the politicalization of crime, the enactment of new laws mandating incarceration and extending confinement for certain categories of offenders, the War on Drugs, and an increase in the number of offenders returned to jails and prisons as parole violators.

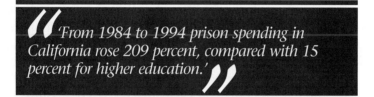

'From 1984 to 1994 prison spending in California rose 209 percent, compared with 15 percent for higher education.'

While policy makers endorse and promote incarcerative and punitive crime control policies, the consequences are not without substantial costs. The financial commitments include the construction and maintenance of facilities; increasing and long-term personnel costs; the expenses of health care for elderly inmates; and the policies, programs, and public services that are being marginalized as governments try to cope with the exorbitant costs of incarceration. For example, [according to Randal C. Archibald] "from 1984 to 1994 prison spending in California rose 209 percent, compared with 15 percent for higher education." Additionally, these policies reflect the pervasive influence that ideology, the media, and politics have in shaping perceptions of and responses to crime and crime control strategies.

The boom in prisons

The good news is that there is no shortage of jobs. In U.S corrections, downsizing, facility closings, and retrenchment are unlikely to occur any time in the foreseeable future. As [Kenneth] Adams has aptly noted, it is a "tremendous bull market" in corrections. [And according to Fox Butterfield,] "Since 1990 alone, the number of prison and jail guards nationwide has increased by about 30 percent, to more than 600,000."

At the beginning of 1999, there were over 1.8 million inmates (645 prison inmates for every 100,000 residents in the United States) under the jurisdiction of the federal, state, and local governments in the United States. While the population of inmates held in jails from 1989 to 1997 increased by an average of about 4.6 percent per year, between 1983 and 1993, the number of jail admissions increased 63 percent from 8.1 million to 13.2 million per year. Interestingly, the number of persons arrested over the same period of time only increased 20 percent (from 11.7 million to 14 million). However, the number of felons sentenced to local jails from 1986 to 1992 increased 90 percent (from 122,400 to 232,300). As a result of these numbers, it is not surprising that in reviewing several jail issues, [Norman] Carlson, [Karen] Hess, and [Christine] Orthmann note that "overcrowding is the most critical concern for today's jail administrators."

Several reasons have been cited to explain the increase in inmate populations and the concomitant overcrowding that has characterized some institutions. A survey of correctional administrators in all fifty states by [Michael] Vaughn found four factors which were identified by 44 administrators as particularly important in understanding why prisons were overcrowded: increased sentence length, the drug problem, the public's desire to get tough on crime, and the legislative response to that demand. . . .

Responses to overcrowding

Federal, state, and local governments have employed a variety of strategies to deal with overcrowding in prisons and jails. In his survey, Vaughn found that responses to overcrowding included increasing the size of existing institutions through expansion projects, double-bunking, increased reliance on community-based correctional services, and new construction. Of these, the most prevalent response is new construction.

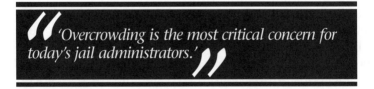

'Overcrowding is the most critical concern for today's jail administrators.'

In 1996, 31 new institutions were opened in 18 different agencies. The new construction resulted in an additional 20,772 beds, at an average cost among 15 agencies of $40,602 per bed. The 1996 construction figures are smaller than those of 1995. In 1995, more new institutions began operations (70) than in each of the previous six years. Cumulatively, the 1990s have witnessed the opening of 343 new institutions.

Although new construction has not surpassed the 1995 peak, prison construction projects continue to flourish. As of January 1997, 61 institutions were being constructed by 22 different agencies resulting in an additional 79,403 beds. The majority of the new prisons (53.4 percent) are medium security suggesting that the demand for prison space does not appear to be to accommodate particularly violent and dangerous offenders.

In terms of expansion projects, 53 facilities were renovated or expanded by 28 different agencies during 1996 adding another 13,912 beds to existing institutions. In 1996, 27 agencies were involved in prison renovation and expansion projects in 118 institutions. If current trends remain unchanged, it is expected that by the year 2001 there will be 1,760 prisons operating in the United States. Clearly, increasing prison populations and demand for prison space will persist for the foreseeable future, and administrators will continue to clamor for additional beds.

One of the few, if only, states to have built enough prison space is Texas. Between 1988 to 1995, Texas added 90,000 state beds at a cost of $2,300,000,000. Before the new construction and renovation of existing institutions could satisfy the demand, Texas was forced to rely on jails for the burgeoning prison inmate population. A number of county jails actually embarked on their own construction projects to help address the demand. Now, Texas is in the position of having too much bed space. As of the spring of 1997, five state facilities are empty waiting for the anticipated growth. The county jail sheriffs in an entrepreneurial manner are advertising their surplus bed space to other states. Some states have decided to avail themselves of Texas's generous offer.

Alternative strategies to address overcrowding

Prison construction is not the only response to prison overcrowding. Front-end strategies include probation and other kinds of intermediate sanctions such as intensive probation, house arrest, electronic monitoring, day reporting centers, and shock probation or split sentences. There were over 3.2 million offenders on probation on December 31, 1996. One of the primary motivations to seeking alternative strategies is the exorbitant costs that are associated with the building and expansion spree. As local institutions, jails are especially affected since [according to Carlson, Hess, and Orthmann] they are "not usually a high priority in the community" and, therefore, lack financial resources to rely on construction strategies. There are also some promising new strategies. [Marc] Mauer reports that Wisconsin has developed "neighborhood probation." Probation officers are assigned to a particular neighborhood and urged to solicit the support of a number of agencies and institutions in the local community to help in providing services and supervising. A number of other communities are experimenting with different forms of "restorative justice" where the victim, offender, and the community are brought together to determine what the appropriate disposition should be.

> *The majority of the new prisons . . . are medium security suggesting that the demand for prison space does not appear to be to accommodate particularly violent and dangerous offenders.*

Vermont has established "reparative probation." In this model, the community boards decide how a probationer will make amends to the community. Probationers selected tend to be first-time offenders who were involved in relatively minor property crimes, who have been carefully screened, and who do not pose a risk to the community.

These kinds of community-based alternatives are designed to deal with nonviolent offenders, including drug offenders. Employing alternative sanctions along with drug treatment and community service might perform the dual function of satisfying the public's demand for tougher sanctions and saving money for other public service projects. In fact, [Joan] Petersilia and [Elizabeth] Deschenes found that approximately one third of nonviolent offenders in Marion County, Oregon, chose prison instead of intensive supervision probation: "For example, inmates viewed 1 year of intensive supervision as equivalent in terms of severity to 6 months in jail . . . ". Clearly, intermediate sanctions and intensive supervision probation are not perceived as lenient treatment by offenders.

States have also employed back-end strategies to cope with

overcrowding. Typically, these involve greater reliance on early release procedures or parole. On January 1, 1997, there were over 500,000 parolees in the United States. Parole practices vary from state to state. For example, in early 1997 California reported the largest number of parolees (100,935); and Maine reported the smallest (57). As previously mentioned, fewer eligible inmates are being paroled than in the early 1990s, and this trend is largely due to the parole board's sensitivity to the public which favors harsher sanctions.

More commonly, states sometimes exercise emergency release procedures when they are under some form of consent decree. Sometimes a court can determine an institutional "cap," but more often it is the legislature which makes the determination. In 1996, ten states and the District of Columbia reported "emergency release programs," all of which were mandated by statute. In five of the reporting states no inmates were released under the provisions in 1996. Such policies typically stipulate that only a fixed maximum number of inmates occupy the prison at any given time.

One of the difficulties with early release strategies is the lack of research that has been conducted to determine their effectiveness. The National Council on Crime and Delinquency evaluated an early release program that was utilized by Illinois. That study found that the program did not increase crime or jeopardize the public's safety. Additionally, the early release policy saved the state millions of dollars by preventing prison overcrowding and all its consequences.

> *One of the primary motivations to seeking alternative strategies is the exorbitant costs that are associated with the building and expansion spree.*

In seeking other cost-effective, safe, and punitive alternatives, [Tony] Fabelo discusses the use of new technology such as "continuous electronic monitoring" and the potential to create "walking prisons." This postindustrial technology is "cheaper than bricks and mortar" but also presents the possibility of widening the net or scope of social control. As prison costs continue to increase, more cost-effective alternatives may help to reduce prison populations and "prisons may become institutions to house only the most violent predator for a long time."

Consequences of long-term incarceration strategies

A serious consequence of continued reliance on long-term incarceration is the commitment of vast sums of money without convincing evidence that such expenditures will pay off in the long run. There are, however, plenty of opportunity costs associated with these strategies. To build and maintain more prisons, the federal, state, and local governments have to secure the revenue from public funds while foregoing other programs. Long after the prisons are built, staffed, and filled with inmates, the public is still required to pay for them at the expense of other services.

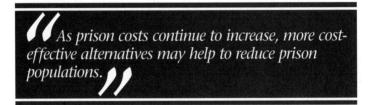

As prison costs continue to increase, more cost-effective alternatives may help to reduce prison populations.

[Phillip] Zimbardo estimates the opportunity costs associated with prison construction by illustrating that one new prison in California is equal to 8,833 new teachers who could have been hired to teach the state's school children or equal to 89,660 children who could be supported to enroll in Head Start programs. Similarly, for what the state of California will spend to incarcerate one third-strike burglar for 40 years, it could have provided two-year community college educations to 200 students. In at least two states, California and Florida, the taxpayers spend more on prison than on higher education.

The imbalance between state funding for prisons versus higher education shows no signs of abating. During the 1980s, California's higher education budget was two and a half times as much as that of corrections. In 1994, the state corrections budget of $3.8 billion was equal to the entire budget allocation for higher education. [In eight years], corrections is expected to consume 18 percent of the entire California budget while higher education will consume less than 1 percent. Consider that in 20 years, California has added one university to the state system while building 21 new prisons.

These kinds of policies are successful at making the public feel as though something is being done about the crime problem. Unfortunately, they camouflage the real issues regarding the antecedents and correlates of crime. They are one more manifestation of a "quick fix" for a complicated societal problem. It will take more than the reactive application of baseball metaphors to address crime in America.

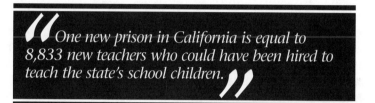

One new prison in California is equal to 8,833 new teachers who could have been hired to teach the state's school children.

When one examines many state expenditures during the last ten years, a common thread emerges. While unprecedented allocations have occurred for corrections, such as the 263 percent increase in Pennsylvania between FY [fiscal year] 1981 and FY 1991, the allocations for the Departments of Education, Health, Welfare, Transportation, and Environmental Resources in Pennsylvania experienced a 75 percent average increase. In fact, the Department of Education received the lowest budget increases (56 percent) over the ten-year period. As the costs associated with current correctional policies continue to escalate, Americans will have to forfeit a great deal.

Postmodern punitiveness

After passing tougher, longer sentences and increasing the reliance on imprisonment, what do politicians and policy makers present to the public to demonstrate and maintain the commitment to punitive ideology? After contributing to [what Wesley Johnson, Katherine Bennett, and Timothy Flanagan call] an "ethos of vindictiveness and retribution" and to [what John Irwin calls] "simplistic ideas about crime and its control," how do legislators raise the deterrent bar of punishment and distract the public from the high costs of imprisonment? [Malcolm] Feeley and [Jonathan] Simon have observed that a "new penology" has evolved which focuses on identifying and controlling populations or aggregates of offenders and managing them through rational processes. This includes "low-frills, no-services control centers" with "new forms of control" based on "risk assessment."

In a continued shift away from "humane treatment of prisoners and the rehabilitative ideal," Johnson et al. also perceive a "no-frills prison movement" which suggests "that prison conditions may continue to worsen." The evidence that courts are becoming more tolerant of violations of prisoners' rights and that lawmakers are reducing and removing "amenities, privileges, activities and opportunities" (e.g., weights, television) for prisoners, supports Feeley and Simon's proposition of this shift in criminal justice focus.

This new wave of offender-prisoner derogation is also consistent with efforts (or the perception of efforts) to contain the tremendous costs of imprisonment. In addition, the increasing market share and profits of private corrections companies suggest that prisons and prisoners have become a "business" that requires efficient cost and management techniques. For example, [David] Shichor has applied [George] Ritzer's McDonaldization thesis[1] to demonstrate this rational, business approach to managing prisons. This is consistent with the "new penology" that incorporates probability and risk, new and efficient techniques of control, a smooth delivery of services, and commitment to the principles of incapacitation. As with the get-tough ideology and policies of the 1980s and 1990s, it appears as though the postmodern penology will generate its own dysfunctions.

No quick fix

The continued reliance on incarceration as a prevailing strategy to reduce crime in America is contraindicative. The opportunity costs and the human costs associated with these policies are too high and allocating additional money into reactive policies masks other issues and public concerns. A successful comprehensive crime control strategy depends on realizing that there is no quick fix to the crime problem.

As [Victor] Kappeler, [Mark] Blumberg, and [Gary] Potter have discussed, presenting simple explanations and quick solutions is part of the crime mythology that is perpetrated on the public. By focusing on sensational, celebrated cases, usually of the "most bizarre and gruesome" nature, the media are giv-

---

1. the process by which the principles of the fast-food restaurant are beginning to dominate more sectors of American society

ing "false impressions of order and magnitude to criminal events." The resulting distortion and frenzy generated by media coverage serves to exacerbate fears of victimization. With an audience emotionally prepared for the worst and an industry focused on instant and dramatic coverage of crime stories, it is not surprising that as [Alfred] Blumstein noted, crime and punishment have captivated public attention. And [according to Peter Greenwood] in spite of declining crime rates, "the continual demands for harsher sentencing, reductions in good-time credits required by truth-in-sentencing statutes, and stricter handling of parole violators all continue to push state prison populations to even higher levels."

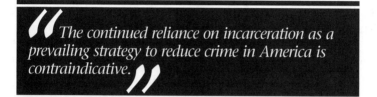

The continued reliance on incarceration as a prevailing strategy to reduce crime in America is contraindicative.

Since the latter part of the 1970s, 15 states and the federal government have eliminated parole boards. In the tradition of hyperreaction and politicalization of crime legislation, politicians have seized on the abolition of parole as part of the "quick fix" to the crime problem. Ironically, three states (Connecticut, Colorado, and Florida) that had decided to abolish parole have now reinstated parole boards [as Butterfield notes] ". . . after finding that abolition did not increase actual time served, because prisons became so crowded that some inmates had to be released early." In fact, according to [Allen] Beck the amount of time being served by inmates is increasing all over the United States and the parole process has no real effect on that phenomenon.

In this regard, Greenwood offers some optimism in observing that "slowly the tide is beginning to turn." Based on his review of recent polls and state legislation, he concludes:

> Many state officials are beginning to recognize that wise investments in early prevention are not only effective ways of reducing crime, but reduce the need for future prison cells as well.

In addition, Greenwood cites evidence that "a large block of voters" understands that building more prisons is not the best policy for dealing with crime.

Criminologists and criminal justice administrators have a role to play in communicating with the public and policy makers. Their testifying before the legislature and the Congress as well as speaking to citizen groups in the community will help to inform the public that these kinds of policies will force economic constraints while not guaranteeing public safety. There is no empirical evidence to support the position that severe punishments alone deter criminal behavior. Not only must the cost and the likelihood of the success of these policies be assessed, but also the fact that their continuation will come at the expense of other programs intended to help children and young people. For example, postrelease consequences could encourage positive, prosocial experiences and limit negative or criminogenic influences.

In discussing the importance of public opinion, retired Oklahoma state corrections professional Jack Crowley observed:

> Public policies on crime and justice, so often enacted as a reaction to public opinion, have led to longer and tougher sentences for offenders, even as those who work in the criminal justice system acknowledge that locking people up does little to rehabilitate them.

Crowley questions why corrections administrators spend so much time reacting to public opinion and public policy rather than working to modify and shape opinions and policies. In the absence of informed, rational policy decisions, the politicalization of crime control has resulted in distorted images of crime and punishment and reactive sentencing and incarceration policies which are not only costly but also counterproductive.

5

Prison Alternatives Can Cut Costs and Improve Public Safety

Daniel L. Lombardo and Robert N. Levy

Daniel L. Lombardo is president and chief executive officer of Volunteers of America, Delaware Valley, a nonprofit, spiritually based organization that has been active in corrections reform for more than a century. Robert N. Levy is director of corrections for Volunteers of America's national office.

There needs to be a nationwide effort to shift the focus of corrections from incarceration to alternative programs that address the special needs of offenders. Most alternative programs are less expensive than incarcerating prisoners, and the savings could be channeled into education and prevention programs. To implement these programs successfully will require an immense amount of collaboration between local communities, the states, and the federal government. Once in place, these programs will benefit all parties involved in the criminal justice system, including offenders, victims, the various corrections agencies, and the local communities.

Volunteers of America, a national nonprofit, spiritually based organization providing local human service programs and opportunities for individual and community involvement, has been a leader in community corrections and corrections reform for more than a century. Maud Booth co-founded Volunteers of America, established the Volunteers Prison League and formed several halfway houses across the nation for offenders returning

Daniel L. Lombardo and Robert N. Levy, "To Confine or Not to Confine," *Corrections Today*, vol. 64, December 2002, pp. 78–81. Copyright © 2002 by the American Correctional Association, Inc. Reproduced by permission.

55

to the community. As practiced more than a century ago, Volunteers of America believes that all people have value and the potential to become law-abiding and contributing community members, and provides an array of correctional services for more than 58,000 people per year. Many of the local offices providing correctional services deliver intensive residential and nonresidential interventions for higher-risk and higher-need federal, state and local offenders.

> *The number of those incarcerated significantly rose while crime rates trended downward nationwide. If crime rates rise, even more will be incarcerated.*

Crowding still exists in many parts of the country at the state and local levels—despite some states recently closing prisons and others considering closures. During the past decade, incarceration grew at an unprecedented rate, while the crime rate started to decline. Some suggest reasons for this rise relate to mandatory and truth-in-sentencing laws and law enforcement or prosecutorial practices that concentrate on arresting and convicting repeat and dangerous offenders subject to more severe penalties, such as mandatory minimums and three strikes laws. Consequently, a greater number of dangerous offenders are receiving longer terms in prison than in the past. However, reportedly, more than half the offenders in prison have been convicted of nonviolent offenses, most of whom could be successfully managed in the community. Aside from more severe laws, political get tough rhetoric influenced many officials to stay the course with prison expansion efforts during the 1980s and 1990s. Additionally, many probation and parole technical violators have had an impact on available prison and jail bed space. In some states, technical violations account for more than 50 percent of state prison referrals annually.

Rising crime rates

Recent reports indicate that the crime rate is leveling off, and in some jurisdictions, slightly increasing. However, the number of those incarcerated significantly rose while crime rates trended downward nationwide. If crime rates rise, even more will be incarcerated. The system needs to aggressively pursue solutions to this issue, especially under tight fiscal times. If addressed aggressively, the system should realize savings, which may free up more tax dollars for education, prevention, health care and housing, not penal institutions. . . .

The Department of Justice, in partnership with several federal departments and state and local governments, recently funded re-entry programs nationwide to assist serious, violent offenders with successful reintegration into the community—a step in the right direction. With more than 600,000 ex-offenders returning home each year, the system must first use funds to address high-risk and high-need repeat offenders for interventions that match the level of risk and need. Properly screened, the highest-risk probationers should present similar risk factors to higher-risk re-entry cases, and will need effective interventions or treatment according to risk and needs. However, to ensure that adequate resources become available long term for higher-risk and higher-need offenders, the justice profession needs to identify low-risk cases early on to link them to community-based services in the least restrictive way.

> *Intensive services intended for addicts would be overkill for periodic marijuana users.*

Consistent with public safety, several jurisdictions fast track low- to medium-risk/need cases into community and restorative justice initiatives, specialized courts and prosecutorial diversion programs, to name a few. Typically, these programs expedite victim restitution collection, community service delivery and, as needed, help program participants get placed in services to address criminogenic needs. The more effectively the justice system processes lower-risk cases in less restrictive ways, the more the system will be able to focus on effective interventions, such as cognitive/behavioral programs for recidivism-prone offenders.

Adopting the least restrictive philosophy helps to avoid net-widening and the tendency to unnecessarily use interventions on lower-risk cases. In most situations, research shows that low-risk offenders would have performed as well or better without a program. Management must safeguard against the development of overly broad eligibility criteria and scrutinize whether the referrals to diversion programs fit the criteria. For example, intensive services intended for addicts would be overkill for periodic marijuana users. . . .

What works

What works is a term used nationally by correctional agencies in reference to principles and practices common to effective public safety and offender programming. Volunteers of America is committed to offering programs, services and policy recommendations based on what works with the offender population. What works research has identified the offender attributes that successful correctional programs must target. Volunteers of America believes that in a true what works system, the mission embraces public safety through offender change, accomplished by risk control and risk reduction through an integrated system of sanctions and interventions. The what works environment means that everyone who has anything to directly or indirectly do with an offender—from entry into the system to completion—is focused on helping that person be successful and is consistent on how he or she does that. . . .

Diverting appropriate offenders

Diversion is being broadly used within this article to include diversion from prison, jail, probation or prosecution. A question that has been posed for many years within the profession is how can the system reserve incarceration for chronic, violent or dangerous offenders? Has the system as a whole improved in this regard? Some would argue yes, stating the mix of those incarcerated contains larger percentages of violent offenders, while others may argue no, reporting that more than half the offenders in prison and jail committed nonviolent offenses. Perhaps both are correct. The system is a work in progress. Regardless, most professionals would agree that too many nonviolent offenders are in prison. . . .

One should take a moment from his or her experience and consider the following: Of the 2 million inmates, could 400,000 (in addition to the 630,000 estimated re-entering this year) be safely released and managed in the community? Of the nearly 4.6 million offenders on community supervision, could another 400,000 be safely transitioned to community health? If so, consider the health system impact. What is needed to meet the challenge?

Systemic changes may be necessary to move lower-risk offenders with special needs out of the system in the least restrictive way, and focus resources on high-risk, re-offense-prone cases. That said, many agencies already have discretion to make changes without having to change rules or laws, for example, specifying which risk or need assessment or cognitive/behavioral program to use. Fortunately, more are making changes to integrate principles of risk, need, responsivity, professional discretion and program integrity into policies, practices and programs. If an agency is undecided, personnel should consider technical assistance from, for example, the National Institute of Corrections. Collectively, these various special needs populations, with disabilities of a physical, emotional and/or mental nature, take up significant prison and jail bed space. Determine whether some could be successfully managed in the community; a shift in the processing of this type of offender toward the front end of the justice system could divert without convicting. In other words, people would accept responsibility for their crimes by agreeing to participate in services as needed. The savings would be enormous.

> *Deciding the fate of non-dangerous special needs cases should not be based on 'difficult to serve,' but rather, 'likelihood to re-offend.'*

Most would agree that the majority of existing correctional institutions were not designed to be a community health delivery system, especially since prison security is the focus. Deciding the fate of non-dangerous special needs cases should not be based on "difficulty to serve," but rather, "likelihood to reoffend." Empirically based risk/need assessment processes can help prevent the system from needlessly incarcerating nondangerous difficult-to-serve populations. If the system is to safely, humanely and effectively use limited correctional resources, then the overwhelming majority of lower-risk special needs cases could be addressed best at the arrest and pretrial stages and diverted from conviction, probation or incarceration. In the long run, this front-end effort could substantially reduce future numbers of those under some form of correctional supervision. . . .

Extensive collaboration is needed

The United States leads the world in incarcerating offenders, totaling more than 2 million inmates—a dubious honor. Most state and local governments have been experiencing correctional budget cuts to offset shortfalls in revenues. This is an opportune time to find ways to cost-effectively use existing correctional funds for offenders who are more likely to threaten public safety, and what works serves this purpose. What works helps justice professionals prioritize limited time, resources and interventions for recidivism-prone offenders. Recidivism reduction helps society improve public safety efforts and prevent victimization. Consistent with the principles of what works, it is time for a systemwide effort to move lower-risk cases, especially with special needs, out of the hands of social control and into community health. Aside from being the right thing to do, diverting low-risk populations out of the system helps reserve correctional resources for the higher-risk to re-offend cases. The long-term objective is to safely curb the growth of a costly prison welfare system.

This challenge is easier said than done. Many have planned for serving special need offenders in corrections and for the higher-risk to re-offend, which will be important to continue. However, as a whole, a concerted effort nationwide does not exist to move out the lower-risk and lower-needs populations into available services in the community, which is needed. Fortunately, federal pilot funding has helped some special needs populations. However, justice and health leaders must work with other committed agency and community stakeholders in a systemwide effort to access more resources for this shift in policy and practice. Extensive collaboration will be needed among the many stakeholders. After all, this is a challenge for most, and a vision to reach. Any explorers?

6

Drug Courts
Are Effective in
Reducing Recidivism

David Cole

David Cole is the Nation's *legal affairs correspondent and the author of* No Equal Justice: Race and Class in the American Criminal Justice System. *He is also a professor at Georgetown University Law Center.*

There are roughly four hundred thousand drug offenders serving prison time. However, prisons do not treat drug abuse and addiction. For that reason, drug courts—a new method of handling drug offenders—have become a popular alternative to incarceration. Drug courts allow nonviolent offenders to complete a drug treatment program in lieu of imprisonment. In these treatment programs offenders receive intensive monitoring and counseling at a cost much lower than that associated with incarceration. Drug courts have also proven effective in reducing recidivism.

Courtroom 202 in the District of Columbia's courthouse looks much like any other inner-city courtroom—windowless, dimly lit, filled with the city's downtrodden and the lawyers who prosecute and defend them. On a Thursday morning, Judge Russell Canan processes a large number of cases in matter-of-fact fashion, slowed only by the failure of defendants and attorneys to appear at their appointed hour.

At 11:30, however, the court is transformed. The judge steps down to the well of the courtroom and welcomes the as-

sembled to a "graduation ceremony." Sitting in the jury box
and the first few rows of the courtroom are thirty men and
women who have successfully completed a lengthy course of
intensive drug treatment. Judge Canan calls each individual
forward, to thunderous applause from their assembled family
and friends. He hands each graduate a diploma and a book,
Acts of Faith: Daily Meditations for People of Color, and, most important, dismisses the criminal cases pending against them.
Each graduate then says a few words. Most thank God, their
families, their treatment counselors and the judge, not neces-
sarily in that order; several give impassioned speeches about finally being drug-free, employed and secure.

Keeping addicts out of jail

This is Washington, DC's drug court, where nonviolent offenders addicted to drugs can avoid prison time if they complete a rigorous course of drug treatment and monitoring. Drug
courts have taken the country by storm. Five years ago there
were only twelve nationwide. [In 1999] there are some 400,
with 200 more in the planning stages. In 1999 Congress ap-
propriated $40 million for drug courts. President [Bill] Clinton
has proposed increasing that to $50 million [in the year 2000].

Nonviolent offenders addicted to drugs can avoid prison time if they complete a rigorous course of drug treatment and monitoring.

Clinton's drug czar, Gen. Barry McCaffrey, calls drug courts
"one of the most monumental changes in social justice in this
country since World War II." Physician Leadership on National
Drug Policy, a bipartisan group of doctors, has strongly endorsed
them. The conservative American Enterprise Institute praises the
courts in a new book, *Drug Treatment: The Case for Coercion*. And
John DiIulio, a conservative criminal justice scholar who has
long advocated tough-on-crime policies, recently celebrated drug
courts in an Op-Ed for the *Wall Street Journal* titled "Two Million
Prisoners Are Enough."

But many on the left remain skeptical of this new approach
to drug law enforcement. Critics assert that drug courts perpet-

uate the criminalization of drugs, widen the criminal justice net, sacrifice due process and privacy rights, and blur important lines between treatment and law enforcement. Many of these criticisms have more than a grain of truth, but in the end they do not outweigh the strongest argument in favor of drug courts: They may finally make it politically feasible to shift drug policy resources from law enforcement to treatment.

Financial costs

Drug courts began as a way to save on the costs of the drug war. In 1980, 19 out of every 1,000 people arrested for a drug crime went to prison; by 1992, that figure had jumped more than 500 percent, to 104. Drug offenders accounted for three-quarters of the total increase in the federal prison population over that period. [In 1999], there are some 400,000 drug offenders in state and federal prisons and jails. At a cost of at least $20,000 a year per inmate, we spend $8 billion annually to warehouse drug offenders.

By contrast, even though sending someone through a drug court program requires intensive monitoring and counseling, it costs only $1,800 to $4,400 a year for nonresidential treatment (residential programs, however, cost significantly more). If drug courts reduce drug abuse and recidivism, they also save on long-term criminal justice and healthcare costs.

Lower recidivism

Drug courts are too new to evaluate definitively, but in theory they ought to work. Virtually all experts agree that the single best predictor of success in drug treatment is the amount of time spent in the program. And few things are more likely to encourage retention than the prospect of doing time behind bars. The most comprehensive survey to date, written in 1998 by Columbia University researcher Steven Belenko, found that 60 percent of drug court participants are still in treatment one year after they began, compared with 10–30 percent of those in noncoercive programs. One of the studies he surveyed found that over a two-year period in Riverside County, California, 13 percent of drug court participants were rearrested, compared with 33 percent of nonparticipants. Belenko also found drug use and recidivism among drug court participants to be lower than among comparison groups both during and after the treatment program. In August 1999 the Urban Institute reached similar results in a sophisticated sixteen-month study of the DC drug courts, finding that the programs significantly reduced drug use during the program and the likelihood of arrest for drug offenses thereafter.

Some criticisms

Yet drug courts continue to generate criticism. Some charge that precisely by making the failed policy of drug criminalization less expensive, drug courts undermine decriminalization efforts. This may well be true, but the nation is so far from decriminalization that this argument seems academic. With or without drug courts, hard drugs will remain illegal for some time. The real question is what we do now with drug offenders—treat them or not.

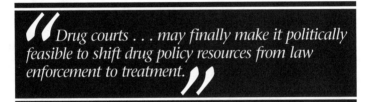

Drug courts . . . may finally make it politically feasible to shift drug policy resources from law enforcement to treatment.

A related concern is that drug courts "widen the net" by capturing an unusually broad array of drug users in the criminal justice system. According to Graham Boyd of the ACLU [American Civil Liberties Union], "drug courts are not actually an alternative to incarceration, because most of those deemed eligible for them would not otherwise face prison time." It's true that many participants picked up for possession or other drug misdemeanors would not have been imprisoned had they chosen to take their chances in the system, but drug court gives them the chance to avoid a criminal record, which might lead to incarceration the next time they're arrested. Moreover, in some jurisdictions, such as the District of Columbia, drug courts are also open to people charged with nonviolent felony offenses who would almost certainly otherwise serve time. In the end, the fact that defendants choose to participate in drug court is a major constraint on net-widening, because they can opt not to enroll if they believe they would be better off otherwise.

Civil liberties advocates point to potential due process problems: Many drug courts require a defendant to plead guilty and waive all trial rights as a condition of entry into the program. They may also require that decision to be made immediately after arrest, when defendants and their lawyers are not likely to be fully informed about the case. This is unfair and also unnecessary. In the DC drug court, for example, defendants do not have to plead guilty, and they may go to trial with all rights intact even if they flunk out of the program. Speedy entry into treatment is desirable, but it should not require surrender of an individual's basic due process rights.

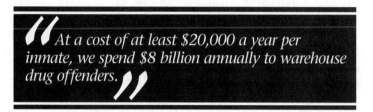

At a cost of at least $20,000 a year per inmate, we spend $8 billion annually to warehouse drug offenders.

Some treatment professionals lament the blurring of lines between the criminal justice system and the medical profession. "Judges are not equipped to make treatment decisions, and treatment providers' first obligation should be to the patient, not the criminal justice system," says Dr. Robert Newman, president of Continuum Health Partners, which manages several hospitals and drug treatment programs in New York. These are valid concerns, but there may also be advantages to the blurring of such lines. Drug courts expose judges and prosecutors to the world of drug treatment, potentially creating a new and especially credible ally for treatment advocates. The introduction of judicial authority and criminal sanctions appears to make treatment programs more effective. And as long as drugs are criminalized, some blurring of treatment and criminal lines is probably inescapable.

Drug treatment advocates are on stronger ground when they criticize the drug courts' failure to allow methadone [a substitute narcotic in the treatment of heroin addiction] maintenance. Drug courts are uniformly based on abstinence, and methadone does not fit that model. Whether drug courts will be able to respond to the increasing prevalence of heroin addiction will turn on their willingness to incorporate methadone maintenance into their programs.

Finally, and probably most fundamentally, critics question whether drug courts and other coercive treatment programs for the criminally accused come at the expense of voluntary treatment spaces. The Office of National Drug Control Policy estimates that half of the 3.6 million people who need treatment in this country cannot get it. Why should treatment be more available to those who have been arrested than to those who have not?

Treatment is less expensive

That's a good question—but there's no solid evidence that drug courts use dollars that would otherwise go to voluntary treatment. If these courts enhance the political appeal of treatment as an alternative to incarceration, they may in fact attract more dollars for treatment, rather than stealing from voluntary programs. Experts have long known that treatment is less expensive than incarceration, yet because our drug policy is driven by what politicians believe the populace will bear, drug policy has emphasized law enforcement. Drug courts, because they demand hard work in treatment, frequent drug testing (with swift and certain sanctions) and regular court appearances, are less susceptible than other treatment programs to being dismissed as soft on crime and therefore more politically acceptable.

Like the book that Judge Canan gives to his graduates, drug courts are still "acts of faith." But because of their broad political appeal, they may finally offer a realistic opportunity to redirect dollars from law enforcement to treatment.

7

Mental Health Courts for Mentally Ill Offenders Are Effective

Lisa Rabasca

Lisa Rabasca is a staff writer for Monitor on Psychology, *a publication of the American Psychological Association.*

Twenty-five to 40 percent of all mentally ill people in America have some form of contact with the criminal justice system. Many of these people bounce in and out of prison because their mental health needs are not properly addressed while incarcerated. Mental health courts were developed as an alternative response to incarcerating nonviolent mentally ill offenders. Relatively new to the criminal justice system, mental health courts diagnose and refer offenders to appropriate treatment programs, including mental health centers, outpatient programs for substance abuse, and various residential treatment programs. So far, these courts have met with success, and as a result, many more mental health courts are going to be developed throughout the nation as an alternative to incarceration.

[In 1998], "Mary," a woman diagnosed with paranoid schizophrenia and accused of loitering, would have waited in jail for 21 days to have her case heard. Then, upon her conviction, she would have served up to six months in a Broward County, Fla., jail.

But thanks to the county's mental health court, instead of serving jail time, she's under court order to receive the mental health care she needs, which in her case includes medication for her schizophrenia, and counseling for substance abuse.

The first mental health court

Mary is one of 1,345 cases helped so far by the mental health court, the first U.S. court to provide treatment to mentally ill defendants who are arrested for nonviolent misdemeanors, such as loitering or creating a public nuisance. The voluntary program offers a service that is often missing in the judicial system: diagnosis of mental illness and follow-up treatment so that mentally ill defendants stop bouncing from homeless shelters to jail to hospitals and back again.

And the program is noteworthy for another aspect. Those who conduct the screenings and determine which cases should be referred to mental health court are doctoral students from the Center for Psychological Studies at Nova Southeastern University. Currently the only graduate psychology program to offer a court-based practicum, Nova requires students to spend 10 to 20 hours at the courthouse each week in addition to their other program requirements, such as coursework in forensic psychology and family and criminal law. Before Nova became involved with the mental health court, no one screened defendants for mental illnesses.

"The students are really an essential operational component of the court," says County Court Judge Ginger Lerner-Wren, who presides over Broward County's mental health court.

The court's success has led a handful of other jurisdictions to establish mental health courts, including King County, Wash., Cook County, Ill., and San Bernardino County, Calif.

Meanwhile, Congress is considering legislation that would provide funding to establish additional mental health courts.

Filling a void

Experts say mental health courts are becoming increasingly important as a growing number of mentally ill individuals are incarcerated in jails and prisons instead of being given mental health treatment. Recent statistics show that:

• Three out of four mentally ill inmates have been sentenced to time in prison, jail or probation at least once prior to their sentence, according to a July 1999 report by the U.S. Bureau of Justice Statistics.

• The same report finds that 16 percent of all inmates in state prisons and local jails suffer from mental illness.

• From 25 percent to 40 percent of America's mentally ill will have contact with the criminal justice system, estimates the National Alliance for the Mentally Ill.

Psychology and law enforcement experts blame this mounting social problem on the drop in mental health services available to people with mental illness after states shuttered their mental health hospitals in the late 1960s and early 1970s. At that time, community treatment centers were expected to fill in the gaps but many couldn't because they lacked the resources to provide services. In recent years, funding for outpatient services has gotten even tighter and people with chronic mental illnesses are more apt to fall through the cracks and end up in jail for petty crimes.

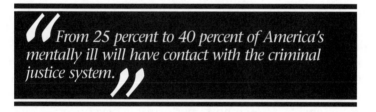

From 25 percent to 40 percent of America's mentally ill will have contact with the criminal justice system.

The need to address this problem is why programs like Nova's are seen as essential.

"Forensic psychology has become one of the hottest areas of the field," says clinical and forensic psychologist Lenore Walker, EdD, professor, coordinator of the forensic concentration and practicum supervisor at Nova. "We're teaching psychology students how to apply their clinical skills to a legal setting."

Walker has worked with the Broward County Public Defender's Office for seven years and helped to bring Nova and the Broward County courts together.

Referrals to mental health courts

Since it began two years ago, 44 students have participated in the forensic program. This year [2000], eight students are participating in the year-long practicum.

Practicum students begin their day early, arriving at the jail at 8 A.M. to screen people who were arrested overnight. The experience gives them an up-close and personal view of the court system and defendants.

"We look at the reasons they're arrested," says Allyson Ruha, a third-year Nova student who is currently in the practicum. "Repeated arrests for disorderly conduct, trespassing and prostitution are often linked to mental health problems."

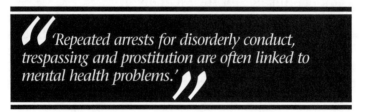

'Repeated arrests for disorderly conduct, trespassing and prostitution are often linked to mental health problems.'

The atmosphere at the jail is initially unsettling, says Ruha, as the defendants haven't showered and those who have been arrested on battery charges are often bruised and bloody.

Before their arraignments, Ruha and other students ask the defendants about prior mental health treatment, whether they've abused drugs or alcohol and if they've had any head injuries. If they identify a defendant with a mental health problem, they alert the public defender and recommend that the defendant be referred to mental health court. If defendants agree to participate in mental health court, students conduct more extensive assessments, performing psychosocial evaluations and sometimes testifying before the judge as to why defendants should receive treatment rather than jail time.

Treatment options

In such cases, the judge usually orders defendants to participate in a treatment program for at least six months. They may be referred to the local mental health center, an outpatient program for substance abuse or a residential treatment program, depending on their needs.

One place defendants may be referred to is OPTIONS, an outpatient program staffed by Nova students. Since January, students have provided individual and group therapy for the 20 women at a treatment center next to the courthouse. OPTIONS can treat up to 40 women with serious mental illness and substance-abuse-related disorders, particularly those who suffer from severe emotional or physical abuse, major depression or post-traumatic stress disorder.

OPTIONS began this year and is funded by a $226,000 grant from the Bureau of Justice Assistance of the U.S. Department of Justice. The program focuses on empowering participants through cognitive-behavioral therapy, individual and group psychotherapy, medication, skills training and self-care activities. For instance, they're encouraged to practice yoga and meditation, learn computer skills and participate in art and group therapy.

Creating more mental health courts

Several members of Congress are hoping to replicate Broward County's mental health court across the country.

Rep. Ted Strickland, PhD (D Ohio), and Sen. Mike DeWine (R Ohio), introduced legislation to create additional mental health courts. Strickland's bill would provide $2 million annually over the next five years to create 25 mental health courts across the nation while DeWine's bill would provide $50 million over the next five years to create 105 mental health courts. Hearings on the proposals are expected to begin this summer.

Both Strickland, a psychologist, and DeWine, a former prosecutor who managed Ohio's prison system when he was the state's lieutenant governor, know firsthand the problems people with mental illness face in jail.

"No one benefits from our current practice of incarcerating nonviolent petty offenders who are in serious need of mental health treatment," says Strickland. "The courts, jail and prisons have become stifled with cases of individuals who are likely to recidivate unless they receive treatment.

Correctional officers are expected to fill the role of mental health professionals when the mentally ill are sent to jail because many of these inmates don't understand why they are there."

8

Teen Courts Benefit Juvenile Offenders

Jeffrey A. Butts and Janeen Buck

Jeffrey A. Butts and Janeen Buck are researchers at the Urban Institute, a nonpartisan economic and social policy research organization. Butts is the director and Buck is the project manager of the Evaluation of Teen Courts project funded by the U.S. Department of Justice.

Teen courts are juvenile diversion programs that serve youths charged with minor law violations such as vandalism, disorderly conduct, alcohol possession, and shoplifting. These courts operate very similarly to traditional courts except that the teens' peers are in charge of the courtroom and serve in various roles such as judge, prosecuting attorney, defense lawyer, and juror. Juveniles who participate in teen courts often have lower rates of recidivism than other youths moving through the juvenile justice system. In addition, teens gain a greater understanding of the law and often a greater sense of personal accountability. Teen courts are considered a viable alternative to punitive punishments.

A dvocates believe teen courts reduce recidivism and increase young people's respect for the law by tapping the power of peer influence. Skeptics worry that teen courts foster net widening[1] and mislead the public with a false aura of legal authority. Nevertheless, state and local jurisdictions throughout the United States seem to be rushing to set up teen courts (also

---

1. increasing the reach of the criminal justice system to include individuals who would not normally be charged with a criminal offense

known as peer courts or youth courts). These programs have obvious appeal for parents and neighbors of troublesome youth. Young people arrested the first time for a minor offense such as vandalism or shoplifting typically receive little attention from the regular juvenile justice system—often nothing more than a warning letter. Teen courts ensure that youth face memorable, albeit unofficial, consequences the first time they are caught breaking the law.

> *When the teen court process moves quickly and decisively . . . it sends a clear message to juveniles that even minor transgressions of the law will not be tolerated by the community.*

Young offenders who appear for hearings in teen court find the lawyer, prosecutor, and jury members are all teenagers. The judge or judges may be young, and teenagers may manage much of what happens in the courtroom. Young offenders rarely get off with a warning in teen court—almost every case ends with some type of sanction or penality. Defendants may be required to repair vandalized property, replace stolen goods, perform community service, or write apology letters to their victims and/or parents. Some may have to return to teen court to serve on juries.

The dominant youth presence in teen court is meant to demonstrate to young offenders that most young people are law abiding, that breaking the law has consequences, and that law breakers are not "cool." When the teen court process moves quickly and decisively—and it is much more capable of doing so than a traditional juvenile court—it sends a clear message to juveniles that even minor transgressions of the law will not be tolerated by the community.

Origins

Precursors to today's teen courts appeared at least fifty years ago. In the 1940s, for example, teens in Mansfield, Ohio, served as judges and attorneys in a "Hi-Y" bicycle court, which heard cases involving minor traffic violations committed by bike-riding juveniles. Infractions like violating the stop sign ordinance or riding at night without reflectors often were punished by requiring offenders to write 300-word essays about traffic laws.

The modern idea of teen courts began to take shape in the 1970s, although they remained relatively obscure and few in number until the mid-1990s. According to some estimates, only eighty teen courts existed in the country as recently as 1993. During the late 1990s, the number of teen courts swelled, in part due to active, financial support from the Justice Department's Office of Juvenile Justice and Deliquency Prevention (OJJDP), which funded the National Youth Court Center (NYCC). There now are more than 800 operating teen courts, with more in planning stages.

Legitimacy

Are teen courts really courts? Although they use courtlike procedures, they are essentially juvenile diversion programs, not courts. They provide a voluntary alternative for young offenders charged with less serious law violations like shoplifting, vandalism, and disorderly conduct. Proceedings in teen court mirror those of the traditional justice system, but youths, not adults, are in charge of the courtroom, serving as judges, prosecuting attorneys, defense lawyers, jurors, bailiffs, and clerks. They are responsible for much of the key decision making in each case, weighing the severity of charges and determining the sanctions.

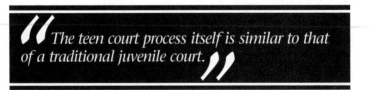

The teen court process itself is similar to that of a traditional juvenile court.

The majority of programs (about 90 percent) require defendants to admit to the charges against them in order to participate in teen court. The court hearings then review the facts of each case, consider mitigating or aggravating circumstances that may be involved, and impose sentence.

In some programs, defendants may dispute the allegations. In these cases, the teen court holds a "trial" to consider the evidence—although the volunteers are not authorized to make findings of legal culpability. When a defendant is able to create sufficient doubt about a case, however, the teen court might be authorized to waive sentencing; in such a case, the youth's participation in teen court would be considered complete. Few jurisdictions provide this option; those that do (e.g., Anchorage, Alaska, and Independence, Missouri) report that youths rarely choose it. Charges are disputed in less than 1 percent of teen court cases.

How they work

The teen court process itself is similar to that of a traditional juvenile court. Defendants typically go through an intake process that includes an interview with an adult program worker. A parent often is required to be present during the intake interview, so this step sometimes occurs just prior to the teen court hearing. The worker explains the teen court process to the offender and parent and ensures that both understand that their participation is voluntary. In most jurisdictions, teen court proceedings and all program records are confidential.

Adults are involved in teen courts to varying degrees. Adults usually administer traditional program management functions such as fundraising, budgeting, staffing, and managing grants and contracts. In some programs, adults also supervise the courtroom during teen court proceedings, and they typically coordinate community service placements in which offenders fulfill the terms of their sentences. In about half of all teen courts, adults serve as judges and youths as attorneys, clerks, bailiffs, and jurors.

> *All teen courts handle relatively minor law violations—shoplifting, disorderly conduct, minor assaults, and alcohol possession are the most common.*

The extent of youth responsibility for teen court hearings depends on the courtroom model used by each program. The NYCC groups teen courts into four basic types: adult judge, youth judge, youth tribunal, and peer jury. The youth judge and youth tribunal models maximize youth involvement because young people perform all courtroom roles, including that of judge. Youth tribunals involve a panel of (usually three) judges that hears cases presented by youth attorneys. The tribunal model eliminates the jury. Hearings following the youth judge model are traditional, with opposing counsel, juries, and a single judge. Adults may assist with courtroom management in these programs, but the teen court hearings themselves are run by youth.

Adult judge programs, used by nearly half of all U.S. teen courts, function much like the youth judge model, except that the judge is an adult who also manages courtroom dynamics. The peer jury model works much like a grand jury: An adult or youth volunteer presents each case to a jury of teens, which questions the defendant directly. The jury members choose the most appropriate disposition, albeit using the guidance and oversight of the adult judge.

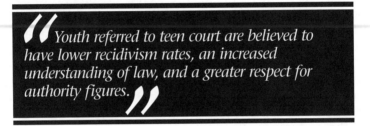

Youth referred to teen court are believed to have lower recidivism rates, an increased understanding of law, and a greater respect for authority figures.

Teen courts usually are administered by or housed within agencies that are part of the traditional juvenile justice system. Law enforcement agencies, juvenile probation, or prosecutor's offices serve as the lead agency for more than half of all teen courts. Only a few are operated by schools, social service agencies, or other private organizations, although the number of school-based programs appears to be growing.

Most teen courts handle relatively few cases. In a recent survey, more than half (59 percent) of teen courts reported handling 100 or fewer cases annually, and just 13 percent handled more than 300 cases per year. In some communities, however, teen courts have become very large. The Anchorage Youth Court, for example, developed into such a large program during its fifteen-year history that it now handles virtually every first-time juvenile offender charged with a nonserious offense. The Anchorage court deals with an estimated 15 percent of the city's delinquency workload, and local judges credit the program with allowing them to focus more closely on other cases involving serious offenses.

Police, courts, and juvenile probation agencies are the primary sources of referrals to teen court. In some jurisdictions, schools also can refer to teen courts, especially individuals with truancy or school behavior problems. All teen courts handle relatively minor law violations—shoplifting, disorderly conduct, minor assaults, and alcohol possession are the most common. Very few programs handle more serious crimes, although some will accept low-level felony offenses on the order of property crimes by first-time offenders.

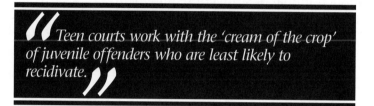

Teen courts work with the 'cream of the crop' of juvenile offenders who are least likely to recidivate.

The dispositions imposed by teen courts include those used by traditional courts: fines, payments of restitution, and community service. In addition, many teen courts offer alternatives like requiring young offenders to attend educational workshops or discussion groups about decision-making skills or victim awareness. Many teen courts require offenders to write formal apologies to their victims; others require offenders to serve on future teen court juries. Failure to comply with these sanctions usually results in a transfer of the case to juvenile or family court for formal handling.

Training

The NYCC recommends that youth volunteers receive an average of sixteen to twenty hours of training before they step into a courtroom. The scope and content of training varies, but the law and legal procedures are the core of most curricula. Some programs recruit adult attorneys to provide training in preparing cases and questioning witnesses for teens acting as attorneys. For example, in the Montgomery County Teen Court program in Rockville, Maryland, adult attorneys attend the program's client-attorney meetings and also observe their teen counterparts in court. Afterward, they provide feedback to youth attorneys about their performance.

Some programs require youth volunteers to pass a written test or assist a more experienced teen attorney before qualifying to serve in a teen court hearing. Youth volunteers with the

Anchorage Youth Court must pass a written "bar exam" before they can appear in court. A bar exam preparation course is taught by local attorneys and focuses on the juvenile justice system and the law, youth court policies and procedures, courtroom roles and responsibilities, case preparation and questioning techniques, and sentencing options. Each participant pays a $15 fee to take the bar exam and can sit for the test as many times as he or she wishes. Many programs, however, do not have such formal or stringent requirements.

Recognizing the need for training standards, the NYCC recently issued guidelines for the content and scope of training curricula.

Effectiveness

Few studies have been published about the effectiveness of teen courts, although their advocates can be very persuasive in describing the benefits. Youth referred to teen court are believed to have lower recidivism rates, an increased understanding of law, and a greater respect for authority figures. Evidence for these claims, however, is largely anecdotal. The expansion of teen courts is still relatively recent, and the reputation they enjoy is derived largely from favorable media coverage and the positive impressions of parents, teachers, court staff, and youth involved in teen court programs. On the other hand, researchers are beginning to find that some of the positive claims for such courts may be valid.

As part of the OJJDP Evaluation of Teen Courts project, the Urban Institute recently reviewed all available studies. Many to date focus on the experiences of participants rather than the subsequent behavior of defendants. Of those that do measure recidivism, many report very low rates of subsequent offenses. Several researchers have found rates for post-program rearrests that range from 3 to 8 percent for the six to twelve months following teen court. A few studies have found recidivism rates in excess of 20 percent. Whether such rates are anomalies is difficult to determine because there are no testing criteria for teen court evaluations.

Skeptics point out that these low recidivism rates are illusory, charging that teen courts work with the "cream of the crop" of juvenile offenders who are least likely to recidivate. Skeptics also worry that the availability of such a popular alternative actually encourages local officials to arrest and process very young and low-risk offenders, thus leading to unproductive net widening. Research findings will impact how courts and policymakers continue to shape the courts' options. . . .

A bright future

The consensus appears to be that teen courts are an option worth pursuing, especially for young people who previously believed courts would judge their first two or three offenses as "freebies" with no meaningful legal consequences. Teen courts help to hold young offenders accountable for illegal behavior, even when the negative consequences are relatively minor and unlikely to result in sanctions from a traditional juvenile court.

Teen court advocates assert that both defendants and youth volunteers benefit from a teen court experience. For defendants, teen court offers the chance to preserve a clean record and to learn from what was perhaps their first serious mistake. For volunteers, teen court provides the opportunity to participate in the larger community and experience the workings of the legal system. For both defendants and volunteers, teen court may impart an increased respect for the law and a greater understanding of the obligations of civil society.

9

nily-Based Therapies Are Successful Alternatives to Juvenile Incarceration

Tori DeAngelis

Tori DeAngelis is a writer living in Syracuse, New York.

Most youth offenders are better served by family-based community programs rather than by group homes or juvenile detention centers. There are several successful programs designed to treat teens by helping them learn to lead crime-free lives. These programs focus on the idea that crime is connected to many other social problems, including mental health issues and drug abuse. Youth work with their parents to help design treatment programs in addition to learning coping skills when faced with negative peer influences. These programs are cost-effective and provide a chance for low- and high-risk youth to survive adolescence.

R esearch shows that delinquent youth fuel each others' bad behavior, yet most young people who commit crimes end up in group homes or juvenile detention centers with like peers.

Three psychologists—Scott Henggeler, PhD, of the Medical University of South Carolina, Patti Chamberlain, PhD, of Oregon Social Learning Center, and James Alexander, PhD, of the University of Utah—take a different tack on treating juvenile delinquency: Using a family and systems approach, they work

Tori DeAngelis, "Youth Programs Cut Crime, Costs," *Monitor on Psychology*, vol. 34, July/August 2003. Copyright © 2003 by the American Psychological Association. Reproduced by permission of the publisher and author.

directly in young offenders' homes and communities to improve their chances of living healthy, crime-free lives while at the same time helping them avoid deviant peers.

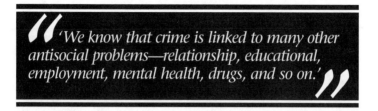

'We know that crime is linked to many other antisocial problems—relationship, educational, employment, mental health, drugs, and so on.'

"The popular perception is, 'These kids are wreaking havoc; let's send them off so they're out of our hair,'" says Henggeler, creator of Multisystemic Therapy (MST), an intensive family-based program now used in 30 states and eight countries. "But it's pretty clear that the vast majority of kids who are locked up don't need to be if you can provide them with good community-based services."

Cutting costs

The programs—MST, Alexander's Functional Family Therapy (FFT), and Chamberlain's Multidimensional Treatment Foster Care Treatment (MTFC)—aren't just feel-good projects: They've been shown in independent analyses to significantly cut crime and reduce costs. In a May 2001 review of 400 studies on crime-reduction programs, for example, psychologist Steve Aos, PhD, of the Washington State Institute for Public Policy, found that in a system that costs up to $64,000 per youth per year, MST saved $31,661, MTFC $21,836 and FFT $14,149 per child per year (a more recent analysis of FFT showed an even greater cost savings in that program). All three interventions also showed major reductions in re-arrests and out-of-home placements compared with conventional treatment.

Because they've shown cost savings, the programs are actually gaining momentum despite a political bent toward incarceration and punishment, the program psychologists add. They received a major boost in 1996, when the University of Colorado at Boulder's Center for the Study and Prevention of Violence (CSPV) chose them as part of its Blueprints for Violence Prevention, a program that identifies the nation's most effective violence-prevention programs. Soon after, the federal Office of Juvenile Justice and Delinquency Prevention (OJJDP) funded CSPV to sponsor replications of the programs through-out the country. As a result, the programs are being more widely disseminated, and there are plans for a pilot project that will combine the three approaches in a triage model for youth entering the system.

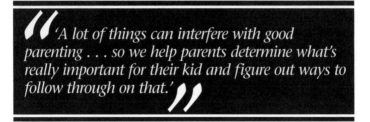

'A lot of things can interfere with good parenting . . . so we help parents determine what's really important for their kid and figure out ways to follow through on that.'

"We know that crime is linked to many other antisocial prob-lems—relationship, educational, employment, mental health, drugs, and so on," comments David Farrington, PhD, professor of psychological criminology at the University of Cambridge and author of "Costs and Benefits of Preventing Crime" (Westview Press, 2001). "Effective programs like these can save money in a lot of different areas."

Unique attributes

Several features distinguish these programs from treatment as usual, their directors note.

Instead of providing individual or group therapy to the young person alone, the programs tailor cognitive, behavioral and family therapy techniques to the needs of teenagers and their families. Youngsters and families help create treatment plans, and parents are coached in parenting skills such as set-ting and enforcing limits and learning to better support their child with attention and praise.

"A lot of things can interfere with good parenting," Cham-berlain explains, "so we help parents determine what's really important for their kid and figure out ways to follow through on that."

The programs also use the concept of risk and protective factors to help determine interventions. An example of a risk factor is parental substance abuse, which for obvious reasons increases the likelihood of poor parenting. To counter this, an FFT clinician, for example, might help the parents find a good substance abuse program or work with families to enhance youth outcomes even if the parents continue abusing substances, Alexander says.

Likewise, a protective factor is positive peer influences, which in turn can help youngsters learn better behavior. "We put a lot of energy into keeping kids out of deviant peer groups and getting them hooked up with prosocial peers in church, school and community groups," Henggeler says, an approach that squares with the research on deviant peers. "It's easier said than done," he adds with a smile. "Kids don't want to leave their friends."

The fact the programs are on-site makes them unique as well, comments psychologist Phillippe Cunningham, PhD, who supervises MST cases in South Carolina.

"We get to see directly what's going on," he notes. "We have the opportunity to reinforce healthy, more adaptive behaviors on the spot, because we get to see the contexts where people get stuck."

Finally, the programs emphasize quality control and outcomes, a focus that has been particularly fostered by Henggeler, whose MST program now includes separate research and dissemination arms. Indiana University psychologist Tom Sexton, PhD, has likewise developed a national dissemination protocol and quality-improvement system so FFT can be disseminated with validity and reliability. Researchers in all three programs regularly conduct evaluations and make changes as data dictate.

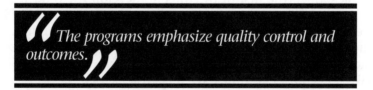

The programs emphasize quality control and outcomes.

The programs differ in key regards as well. MTFC, for example, first places youngsters with foster families, who are coached in parenting and social-learning skills. At the same time, the youngster's family of origin learns the same techniques so they're ready when the youngster returns home. Henggeler's program is likewise intensive, but immediately begins to work with the child's family and in his community, providing around-the-clock assistance as needed. Alexander's approach is more short-term and proceeds through three distinct stages, from motivating families to teaching new skills to linking them with community supports. The programs last for different periods of time and cost more or less money as a result.

But they have more in common than not, program psychologists emphasize. "We came up with the programs independently," says Henggeler, "but we all had access to the same knowledge base. If you look at the Blueprints project, you see that only three programs out of 600 were selected because they had positive outcomes related to juvenile offenders. That gives you a good idea of what works and what doesn't."

New directions

The programs are building on their successes in several ways. Later this year [2003] the Annie E. Casey Foundation plans to run a pilot project that will combine the three approaches in a single setting. The aim is to see if they can work complimentarily to provide effective treatment for young people entering the system.

In addition, program psychologists are expanding the types of clients they serve. Henggeler's team, for example, is studying ways to adapt MST to juvenile sex offenders, teens from abusive families and young people with serious mental health problems. Alexander, Sexton and FFT Dissemination Director Doug Kopp are applying FFT to increasingly diverse populations such as underage sex offenders in Anchorage, Alaska. Meanwhile, Chamberlain has focused her recent efforts on girls.

Alexander, the first of the three to develop the model, says the approaches give hope to youngsters and their families who face higher odds than most, including poverty and family dysfunction. "We tend to act as though these things are a death sentence," Alexander says. "These programs offer ways for people to make it even though they have huge risk factors."

10

Restorative Justice Benefits Victims and Offenders

Jeff Anderson

Jeff Anderson is an author who has written about prison issues.

Restorative justice is a successful alternative to sending offenders to prison. Imprisonment often does little to rehabilitate the criminal or repair the damage done to the victim and the community. Restorative justice involves creating a dialogue between the victim, the offender, and the community to repair the harm caused by the crime. Together these parties determine the punishment and restitution. This method supports the victims and allows them to be part of the justice process, increases offender awareness of how their actions affect others, and makes certain that the offenders get the education or treatment they need to avoid further criminal activity.

R are is the criminal who takes into account the effect of his actions on his victims.

But what if he did? What if he could look into a crystal ball and see the impact of his crimes on both his victim and the community? If, for even a moment, he stopped to consider the human cost of his actions on his victim(s)—the pain, the anguish, the feelings of powerlessness and helplessness, the sense of violation—it's a good bet that only the most callous among us would follow through and still commit their crimes.

Unfortunately, most would-be criminals don't do that. In

Jeff Anderson, "Restorative Justice: Making Things Right," *The Prison Mirror*, vol. 112, May 1999. Reproduced by permission of the Minnesota Correctional Facility-Stillwater.

fact, it is an offender's very ability to ignore these costs—to temporarily (or in some cases, permanently) turn off our sense of empathy and compassion—that allowed many of us to do what we did.

Just as unfortunate, however, is society's willingness to throw away so many of its citizens without a second thought. For the better part of three decades, our answer to the rising tide of crime was to simply lock people up. But while sending criminals to prison may satisfy the victim and the community's thirst for retribution, it does little to actually repair the damage done or to restore the peace of mind of the victim or the community. Even victims who see their victimizers locked away in prison are often left with an empty, unsatisfied feeling; a feeling that what was taken from them was never replaced. And in regard to younger offenders in particular, the pattern was becoming all too obvious and familiar: Today's "younger and less violent" offenders were quickly turning into tomorrow's more serious criminals.

> *Sending criminals to prison . . . does little to actually repair the damage done or to restore the peace of mind of the victim or the community.*

Frustrated by the sense of emptiness and lack of resolution expressed by victims (and its ineffectiveness in reducing the rates of incarceration and recidivism), the state of Minnesota began searching for alternatives to the expensive and largely unsuccessful proposition of locking people up.

Restorative justice

Looking to stem the tide, so to speak, the Department of Corrections in 1994 "established a department unit to support the implementation of restorative justice concepts throughout the state," the first state in the nation to do so. As part of the initiative, the department created a full-time position to facilitate the implementation of restorative justice programs in communities throughout the state. Unlike the impersonal, punitive approach that has become the cornerstone of our current criminal justice system, restorative justice philosophy differs in that it emphasizes crime as a violation of the victim and the community—not the state—and forces offenders to confront the human and emotional consequences of their actions. Likewise, it is the victim and the community that offenders become accountable to.

> *Restorative justice philosophy . . . emphasizes crime as a violation of the victim and the community—not the state.*

Restorative justice provides an alternative "framework" to our conventional criminal justice system. One of its most basic tenets is the belief that victims should be central to the process of justice; thus, they are offered an expanded role. And while prison or other forms of punishment are not excluded, personal responsibility and restitution are emphasized. All the affected parties—the victim, offender and members of the community—become active participants in the process and together, they determine what the appropriate means of punishment and restitution should be. Opportunities to participate in restorative justice programs are expanding, though they are currently used primarily for less serious offenses and as a diversion from prosecution for juveniles.

According to Kay Pranis, the restorative justice planner for the Department of Corrections, restorative justice concepts represent a profound shift in corrections philosophy.

"It is an approach to crime, and our response to crime, that focuses not just on punishing the offender, but on repairing and healing the harm. It defines accountability as taking responsibility for your behavior rather than punishment.

"Restorative justice is not about what we do to the offender but rather, what does the offender need to do to repair the damage?"

As opposed to offenders simply going to court and answering to a judge, restorative justice is a holistic approach that involves the entire community, including schools, churches, courts, corrections and law enforcement agencies and citizens.

Restorative justice doesn't just punish the offender; it gives the victim and the community a voice that they otherwise wouldn't have. And because of that, Pranis said, victims express a much higher degree of satisfaction with the outcomes of a restorative justice process than with the conventional criminal justice system.

"Being victimized is a very disempowering experience," said Pranis. "Often, they lose faith in their entire community, they stop trusting themselves and their instincts, they feel isolated and alone, cut off. Restorative justice helps give them back a sense of power over their own lives.

"Overwhelmingly, the sentiment expressed to me by victims is a desire to make sure that it doesn't happen to anyone else; their concern is that the offender gets the help they need—education, treatment, whatever it takes—in order to ensure that no one else is victimized."

Minnesota is a pioneer in the field, becoming the first state in the nation to incorporate restorative principles into their mainstream corrections system. "Minnesota gave restorative justice legitimacy across the nation," said Pranis. "Now, other people in other states look at restorative justice and they take it seriously. I think Minnesota has had a huge impact nationwide."

Community empowerment

While the problem of crime and punishment has been primarily handed over to the courts, Pranis believes that the most effective solutions lie in the communities themselves. And unlike our conventional criminal justice system, restorative justice principles empower the entire community.

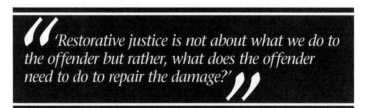

'Restorative justice is not about what we do to the offender but rather, what does the offender need to do to repair the damage?'

"Communities are anxious to get involved and take control of their own fate," she said. "Relationships are the most powerful force in shaping human behavior and restorative justice helps to build relationships between the offender and the community. Change comes about when offenders realize that people really do care about them.

"Our current response (to crime) reinforces the depersonalization that exists between offenders and the community," she continued. "In most cases, offenders never even have to answer for what they did. Silence is encouraged from the beginning, the lawyers do all the talking, there are judges and rules and procedures . . . everything is by the book legal; it's so impersonal. Offenders never have to confront the emotions of what they did."

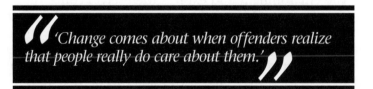

'Change comes about when offenders realize that people really do care about them.'

One of the distinct advantages of restorative justice over our conventional system is that it offers an opportunity for direct interaction between the victim, the offender and affected members of the community. Typically, offenders are not even aware of the emotional impact of their crime on their victims, so inevitably, they commit even more crimes. But faced with the human cost of their actions, offenders become less likely to re-offend. It's also more likely that the involved parties will come to a more satisfactory resolution.

Encouraging results

And so far, they have been right. Though restorative justice is a relatively recent phenomenon, the early results are encouraging.

Mark Umbreit, who is the director of the University of Minnesota's Center for Restorative Justice and Mediation and a leading authority on restorative justice, recently conducted a large multi-state study of victim-offender mediation programs with juveniles. The two-year study showed the following:

- Of 3,142 cases referred to the study, 95 percent resulted in a successfully negotiated restitution agreement.
- Victims who participated in mediation were more likely to be satisfied with the justice system (79 percent) than similar victims who went through the normal court process (57 percent).
- After meeting with the offender, victims were significantly less fearful of being revictimized.
- Offenders who met with their victims were far more likely to successfully complete their restitution agree-

ment (81 percent) than similar offenders who didn't participate (58 percent).
- Fewer offenders who participated in victim-offender mediation recidivated (18 percent) than similar offenders who did not (27 percent). Furthermore, participating offenders' subsequent crimes tended to be less serious.

With restorative justice, the parties are able to get together in a safe environment and express themselves concerning the incident. They are able to talk about what happened, how they were affected and finally, what needs to be done to make amends. Participation is strictly voluntary (there is no mandating) and offenders must accept responsibility for their crimes and agree to follow through with the terms of their agreement before they are allowed to participate. It is a process that is proving to achieve more positive results and to offer more satisfactory outcomes for everyone involved.

Different objectives

Pranis also explained that the objectives of the restorative justice process differ from our normal criminal justice system.

The ideal of restorative justice (and Kay's vision) is corrections intervention that leaves communities stronger than before; neutralizing people in prison doesn't accomplish that. This, she believes, can be more effectively done by emphasizing the following: 1) Focusing on offenders repairing and restoring the harm (to whatever degree possible); 2) Supporting victims and allowing them to be part of the decision-making process; 3) Increasing offender awareness of how their actions affect others; 4) Making sure that offenders leave the system better off than when they entered; and 5) Involving all of those who were most affected. Pranis also believes that corrections are most effectively handled by communities at the local level.

'Offenders are us. . . . They are products of their environment and often, they mirror what is wrong with the community.'

Though only . . . introduced [in 1999] on a state-wide level in Minnesota, restorative justice concepts have spread like wildfire. As part of the Department of Corrections restorative justice initiative, services are now available in dozens of Minnesota counties. . . . And if Pranis has her way, restorative justice services will eventually become available in every part of the state.

Believing that the problem of crime can be most effectively resolved by communities working in conjunction with the criminal justice system, Kay would like to see restorative justice options such as peace circles and family group conferencing available in most cases. Justice she believes, should not be of the cookie cutter variety but about forgiveness, healing and restoration.

Pranis also believes that it's possible for prisons to be run restoratively, as well. This, she said, could be done by emphasizing a fundamental respect for human dignity and providing opportunities for inmates to make amends while they are incarcerated. Community service can take place even in prison, and programs should be made available that will help offenders remain accountable to their victims and connected to their communities. Victim impact groups and other programs that help teach proper thinking and behavior would also be helpful.

Connecting with offenders

Another important aspect of restorative justice that is often overlooked by our conventional system is the road traveled by an individual that led him or her to a life of crime. In many cases, Pranis found, offenders have themselves been victims.

"Once you sit in a (sentencing) circle and see what the offender has gone through," she said, "all the easy answers go away. Not that they aren't responsible for their actions, but often there are other factors involved that we don't always see."

Oftentimes, offenders are seen as castoffs and outsiders from their community but according to Pranis, it's important that individuals remain members of their community and find a way to stay connected. She used an environmental analogy to illustrate her point.

"It's like an empty bottle or any other type of waste," she said. "We can't just treat it like garbage. We have to find a way to re-incorporate, re-cycle or re-integrate it. If we don't it will eventually come back to poison us.

"Offenders are us," she concluded. "They are products of their environment and often, they mirror what is wrong with the community. If we look real close, there are lessons to be learned."

11

Shame Punishment Is an Effective Alternative to Incarceration

Aaron S. Book

Aaron S. Book is an associate with the law firm Reed, Smith, Hazel & Thomas, located in the Washington, D.C., area. He served as a senior articles editor for the William and Mary Law Review *from 1998 to 1999.*

Shame punishment has existed since the beginning of recorded history. It is a less severe form of punishment than imprisonment and serves as an effective alternative to incarceration, which often reinforces criminal behavior. Shaming usually involves the offender undergoing some form of public humiliation, such as having to wear a sign saying, "I am a thief." Being humiliated forces the individual to acknowledge his or her crime in the face of public scrutiny. Shame punishments are often given alongside community service—allowing the offender to try to repair some of the damage he or she has caused in the community while also forcing the offender to recognize his or her inappropriate behavior.

Daniel Alvin stood before Georgia State Court Judge Leon M. Braun, Jr., to receive his sentence after being convicted of eight counts of theft. Alvin, husband to a pregnant wife and father of disabled eight-year-old twins, convinced eight victims to hand over money for Atlanta Hawks basketball tickets and a charter bus ride to the game. The tickets and the bus ride never materialized. The police did, however, and charged Alvin with theft by taking.

Aaron S. Book, "Shame on You: An Analysis of Modern Shame Punishment as an Alternative to Incarceration," *William and Mary Law Review*, vol. 40, February 1999, p. 653. Copyright © 1999 by the College of William and Mary. Reproduced by permission.

Judge Braun decided to offer Alvin a choice: he could spend six months behind bars, or he could spend five weekends in jail and walk around the Fulton County Courthouse for a total of thirty hours wearing a sign that read "I AM A CONVICTED THIEF." Alvin chose the second option and dutifully carried his sign around the courthouse to the honks and cries of passersby. Although the sentence caused Alvin significant embarrassment in his community, he spent minimal time in jail, and his family stayed together.

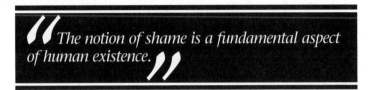

The notion of shame is a fundamental aspect of human existence.

Judge Braun's decision to offer Alvin an alternative to incarceration represents a growing trend among sentencing judges. Frustrated with the ineffectiveness of traditional forms of punishment, judges are imposing sentences of shame upon convicted criminals more frequently. Ranging from the mundane to the Byzantine [intricately involved], such sentences are not without controversy.

Professor Dan Kahan, a supporter of shame punishment, believes that "[s]haming is a potentially cost-effective, politically popular method of punishment" that will enjoy future success because people "want more from criminal punishment. They want a message. They want moral condemnation of the offender." On the other side of the debate, Mark Kappelhoff of the American Civil Liberties Union criticizes shame punishment as "[g]ratuitous humiliation of the individual [that] serves no societal purpose at all." Mr. Kappelhoff adds that "there's been no research to suggest [that] it's been effective in reducing crime." While the issues are far from settled, there is no doubt that shame is receiving national attention. . . .

The evolution of shame

The notion of shame is a fundamental aspect of human existence. It is no surprise, therefore, that early forms of punishment focused on the idea of shame. Imposition of shame punishment can be traced back to the dawn of civilization. In its earliest forms, shame punishment was based on one's essential attachment to society and civilization. Tribes, communities, and villages were essential to life. Indeed, in early times, the community was synonymous with life itself. One of the harshest forms of punishment was banishment from one's community. Such punishment ensured a life of hardship or, perhaps, death.

Shaming continued to evolve throughout Europe with the invention of bizarre and horrifying methods of public torture that typically ended in the death of the accused. These methods traveled to America where, thankfully, they became less brutal, but no less humiliating. For relatively minor offenses, a citizen received an admonition—he appeared before a magistrate to be publicly and formally denounced. More serious offenders were sent to the pillory or stocks. The most egregious offenders faced the brutish shaming ritual of branding or mutilation, thus [according to scholar Adam Jay Hirsch] "fixing on [the offenders] an indelible 'mark of infamy' to warn the community of their criminal propensities." For example, in Williamsburg, Virginia, an individual convicted of thievery was nailed by the ear to the wooden brace of the pillory for a period of time that depended upon the seriousness of his offense. After the offender served his sentence, the authorities ripped him from the pillory without first removing the nail. The individual was thus "ear-marked" as a criminal offender for the remainder of his life.

The efficacy of shaming began to wane as society became more mobile.

[According to French philosopher Michel Foucault] gradually, this "gloomy festival of punishment" began to lose favor as America became a more progressive society. Punishment evolved from the physical to the psychological, as citizens and legislators began to embrace the philosophy of institutionalized punishment. As Americans moved westward, settlers realized the effectiveness of jails and prisons for housing society's offenders. The efficacy of shaming began to wane as society became more mobile. America was expanding rapidly, and individuals were no longer confined to their town or village. As a consequence, a criminal shamed in one community could easily pick up and move to another and enjoy a fresh start. By the dawn of the twentieth century, many courts had rejected shame as a useful form of punishment. Shame then experienced a period of dormancy until the late twentieth century, when it enjoyed a creative renaissance in a more enlightened form.

Beginning in the mid-1970s, trial judges began to reincorporate shame into their judicial arsenal. Sentences incorporating shame punishment have encountered varying degrees of acceptance at the appellate level. The practice of assigning shame-related punishment to offenders has continued to the present, with judges developing new methods of punishing criminals without having to send them to prison. . . .

The warning signs

In the 1997 case of *People v. Meyer*, an Illinois trial court convicted a sixty-two-year-old defendant of aggravated battery after he struck and kicked another man who came to his farm to return some borrowed auto parts. At the sentencing hearing, the court heard evidence of aggravating and mitigating circumstances in order to determine the proper punishment. After considering all of the testimony, the lower court judge sentenced the defendant to probation instead of prison. The conditions of probation included restitution to the victim, payment of a fine, and, among other things, placement "at each entrance of his property [of] a 4' × 8' sign with clearly readable lettering at least 8" in height reading: 'Warning! A Violent Felon lives here. Enter at your own Risk!'" . . .

In *State v. Burdin*, the Supreme Court of Tennessee required a defendant convicted of sexual battery to place a sign in his front yard notifying the community of the nature of his crime. In addition to a suspended sentence, as a condition of confinement, the court required the defendant to erect a 4' × 8' sign reading "Warning, all children. Wayne Burdin is an admitted and convicted child molester. Parents beware." The court mandated that the defendant place the sign in the front yard of his residence where he lived with his mother. . . .

Drunk driver notification

In *People v. Letterlough*, the New York Court of Appeals struck down a probation condition requiring a convicted drunk driver to affix a sign to his license plate notifying the public of his offense. In 1991, the State of New York convicted Roy Letterlough of driving while intoxicated. It was his sixth conviction for an alcohol-related driving offense. His initial sentence resulted from a plea agreement and included five years of probation, payment of a $500 fine, and alcohol treatment directed by the Department of Probation. When Letterlough arrived for his formal sentencing, the court imposed an additional condition not stipulated in the prior plea agreement. The court mandated that if Letterlough ever reobtained a license during his five-year probationary period, he would have to affix a sign to his license plates that read, in fluorescent letters, "convicted dwi." The sentencing judge warned Letterlough that he would violate probation and face resentencing if he failed to use the signs.

The sentencing judge carefully specified that the sign should be removable so as not to penalize unfairly innocent drivers, such as family members, who might use the same car as Letterlough. In addition, he articulated a clear rationale for the unusual probation condition, stating:

> "I only wish to warn the public of this and only have this sign apply to this Defendant. . . . This gentleman is 54 years of age and I do not wish to be the one that opens a newspaper and sees that this gentleman has caused an accident that has taken an innocent person's life because I did not do something that either warns the public or treated his problem. I hope to be doing both.". . .

In the case of *Lindsay v. State*, the Florida District Court of Appeals upheld a probation requirement that a convicted drunk driver place an advertisement in a local newspaper describing his crime. The trial court convicted Charles Lindsay of drunk driving after he ran into the back of a police patrol car while drinking beer. It was Lindsay's first conviction for drunk driving, and the sentencing judge intended it to be his last by requiring Lindsay to place his picture in the local paper along with the details of his offense. . . .

A less severe punishment

Shame punishment is less severe than corporal punishment. No measurable physical pain is inflicted on the offender—which indicates that the punishment is not cruel—nor is the offender subject to anything but temporary and mild emotional distress. Such distress presumably is far less than would be experienced if the offender were forced to serve a prison sentence.

Shame punishment also is not unusual. It is, rather, a creative alternative to traditional, and arguably ineffective, modes of punishment that draws its essence from American historical tradition, and has reemerged in a less severe and more effective form.

Does shaming work?

Regardless of whether shame punishments would survive an Eighth Amendment challenge or any other judicial analysis, courts should not impose such punishments unless there is some probability that they will rehabilitate criminal offenders. If such punishments do not work, implementing them would be a waste of judicial time and resources, and would result in placing a convicted offender in a position where he could offend again. While there is no empirical data analyzing the effectiveness of shaming as punishment, there is evidence that shaming is an effective and creative means of keeping some offenders out of the prison system while simultaneously giving them a chance at rehabilitation. This evidence takes on two forms.

First, the psychological literature indicates that shaming works. From a psychological perspective, shaming shapes behavior from childhood to adulthood. Because shaming affects humans at a clinical, psychological level, it could work on the punitive level. Second, a more common-sense approach posits that, because the prison system is not effectively solving the crime problem in America, society must explore alternatives that give offenders a chance at changing their ways without subjecting them to an environment that only can reinforce their criminal behavior. . . .

The psychological aspect: Shame is good

In general, one can assume that people have an aversion toward the commission of crime. In contemporary society, there are more law-abiding people than criminals, [according to professor John Braithwaite,] "People comply with the law most of the time not through fear of punishment, or even fear of shaming, but because criminal behavior is simply abhorrent to them." The development of an anti-crime attitude by the majority of the population originates with shaming early in life.

Almost everyone, at one time or another, must face some

type of shame punishment. Many parents punish their children's simple transgressions with spankings, lectures, and banishment to the child's room so the child can reflect on his or her conduct. Such simple shaming techniques are the foundation of conscience, shaping human attitudes toward the unthinkableness of crime. Parental shaming techniques are effective in that they serve to ingrain an automatic anxiety response in the individual that continues into adulthood.

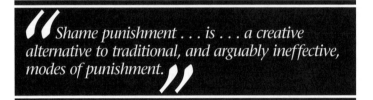

Shame punishment . . . is . . . a creative alternative to traditional, and arguably ineffective, modes of punishment.

Verbal shaming frequently accompanies physical shame punishment. Parents often tell children that they are "bad" or "naughty" for doing something wrong. [According to Braithwaite,] "This verbal labeling is the key to a process of generalization that groups together a variety of types of misbehavior . . . that all elicit conditioned anxiety; in time the generalization proceeds further, with the more abstract concept of 'crime' being defined as 'naughty' or 'evil.'" If one accepts this argument, one also would be likely to accept the further assertion that conscience is a trait acquired through a variety of shaming techniques imposed in differing degrees by the family throughout the developmental process of the child.

As an individual progresses to adulthood, the specter of parental shame tends to diminish as the more powerful adult human conscience takes over to control actions. As John Braithwaite describes:

> In the wider society, it is no longer logistically possible, as it is in the nursery, for arrangements to be made for punishment to hang over the heads of persons whenever temptation to break the rules is put in their path. . . . Unlike any punishment handed down by the courts, the anxiety response happens without delay, indeed punishment by anxiety precedes the rewards obtained from the crime, while any punishment by law will follow long after the reward. For most of us, punishment

by our own conscience is therefore a much more potent threat than punishment by the criminal justice system.

For most individuals, therefore, shame and conscience are inextricably intertwined both to deter crime and to impose a self-penalty on those who commit crimes. There are, however, those who commit crimes despite the existence of conscience. The conscience of those individuals may have failed with respect to their criminal acts. In these circumstances, shame punishment has the greatest potential effect. [Braithwaite states,] "[S]haming can be a reaffirmation of the morality of the offender by expressing personal disappointment that the offender should do something so out of character. . . ."

> *'For most of us, punishment by our own conscience is . . . a much more potent threat than punishment by the criminal justice system.'*

Shame can function as both an effective punishment of criminals and a tool for the rehabilitation of offenders. It can be a powerful tool indeed, but only in a society that has a need for it and wields it properly. . . .

The need for shaming

Shaming as a form of punishment works to rehabilitate criminal offenders. The question that remains is whether shaming punishment is necessary. Shaming is a rational and evidently much needed alternative to the traditional choice of prison and probation. Many Americans have lost confidence in the criminal justice system: a 1997 Gallup Poll indicated that forty percent of Americans have "very little" or no confidence in the system. Only twenty percent had "a great deal [or] quite a lot" of confidence. These numbers are a disturbing comment on criminal justice, especially considering that Americans ranked crime and violence as the most important problems facing the country. Similarly, Americans have lost faith in their state prison systems: in 1996, over seventy-four percent of Americans had only "some" or "very little" confidence in their state prisons.

America's opinion of the probation system is equally low. In response to suggestions to reduce prison overcrowding, only slightly more than twenty percent of Americans believed that parole boards should be given more authority to release offenders early. Less than sixteen percent felt that regular probation supervision was "very effective" as an alternative to prison. Between 1980 and 1993, the United States increased per capita expenditures for the criminal justice system by more than 308%. During that same period, state governments increased their direct expenditures on correctional institutions by over 368%. As evidenced by their dissatisfaction with the prison system, Americans perceive that they are getting less for their tax dollar. To highlight the frustration Americans feel, in 1996, sixty-seven percent of Americans indicated that they thought government allocated too few funds to halt the rising crime rate effectively.

America, therefore, needs alternatives to a prison system perceived as ineffective in preventing crime and rehabilitating offenders. The data show that many Americans would favor alternatives to prison, such as shaming. Over eighty-nine percent of people polled favored the imposition of local programs that would keep nonviolent and first-time offenders out of prison and permit them to remain active members of their communities. While the poll did not specifically mention shaming, such punishments would fall within the definition specified by the pollsters because an essential feature of these punishments or programs is to permit offenders to remain part of their community.

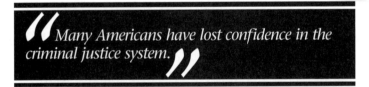

Many Americans have lost confidence in the criminal justice system.

Shame punishment is a particularly attractive option considering the number of nonviolent offenders in the criminal justice system. In 1993, for example, the U.S. district courts convicted 53,435 defendants. Of these, only 3,077, or 5.76%, were found guilty of committing violent offenses. The rest were convicted of nonviolent offenses. This is not to say that all nonviolent offenders would be suitable for shame punishment. The candidate pool is very large and there are presumably thousands who would benefit from nontraditional punishments.

Consider that over 20,000 of the total convictions in U.S. district courts mentioned above were for drug-related charges. Another 13,000 or more were for offenses such as bribery, perjury, liquor, gambling, and weapons offenses. Moreover, out of the total of those convicted, almost 19,000, or 48.2%, had no prior criminal record. Pending some basic evaluation at the trial court level, many of these individuals might be ideal candidates for shame punishment because of the nonviolent nature of their crimes.

The American public is frustrated with the current criminal justice system, which it perceives as ineffective. This is true despite skyrocketing budgets devoted to that system. The vast majority of the population favors some type of alternative punishment that would keep first-time offenders out of prison and, hopefully, create productive and law-abiding citizens. The prison population consists of primarily nonviolent offenders. Of these, many are first-time offenders. Subjecting these offenders to shame punishment instead of incarceration may prevent them from becoming recidivists.

12

Electronic Monitoring Is a Popular Alternative to Imprisonment

Scott Vollum and Chris Hale

Scott Vollum and Chris Hale are doctoral students in the College of Criminal Justice at Sam Houston State University in Huntsville, Texas.

Electronic monitoring is a form of community supervision that requires offenders to wear an electronic device on their bodies so correctional staff can track their movements. Electronic monitoring is one of the most popular alternatives to incarceration. The public as well as the correctional system began to embrace electronic monitoring as a result of the get tough on crime attitude prevalent in the past two decades. However, there is no conclusive evidence to support the effectiveness of electronic monitoring. Despite the fact that it may not save money or reduce recidivism or alleviate prison crowding, electronic monitoring will likely continue to be a popular alternative to prison.

Prison and jail populations rose considerably during the 1980s and 1990s. According to Stephen Donziger [author of *The Real War on Crime*], "Since 1980, the United States has engaged in the largest and most frenetic correctional buildup of any country in the history of the world." At the beginning of this new millennium, there is no sign that such trends are waning. In fact, as of year-end 2000, 6.5 million people were under some form of correctional supervision. Since 1980, the U.S.

Scott Vollum and Chris Hale, "Electronic Monitoring: A Research Review," *Corrections Compendium*, vol. 27, July 2002. Copyright © 2002 by the American Correctional Association, Inc. Reproduced by permission.

prison and jail population increased by more than 240 percent to more than 2 million people as of mid-year 2001. Additionally, as the 20th century drew to a close, there were more than 4.6 million people on probation or parole in the nation.

The ramifications of these numbers are very real. In the 1980s and early 1990s, 600 new state prisons were built and state expenditures increased by 325 percent for prison operations and by 612 percent for prison construction. Despite the frantic construction of new prisons and the vast increases in spending, adequate housing for offenders became increasingly rare. Currently, jails and prisons continue to experience crowding and resources are still strained. In addition, growing caseloads have become more and more overwhelming for probation and parole officers. As the weight of these trends impacted the criminal justice system, it became increasingly necessary to examine alternative sanctions to provide some form of relief.

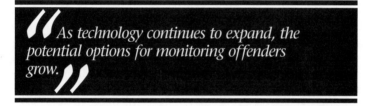

As technology continues to expand, the potential options for monitoring offenders grow.

Electronic monitoring—one technique among numerous alternative sanctions proposed in the 1980s and 1990s—emerged and remains a popular and increasingly used measure today. Also, the number and variety of techniques used to electronically monitor offenders have proliferated in recent years and the offender populations for which they are being implemented have become more diverse. More recently, electronic monitoring has become a popular alternative sanction and form of community control internationally, flourishing in the United Kingdom. Among the many alternative correctional programs and techniques proposed, electronic monitoring stands today as one of the few persistent alternatives. . . .

What is electronic monitoring?

Electronic monitoring often is referred to as "house arrest" and serves to keep offenders in the community, and more important, out of prison or jail while, at the same time, restricting their movement. It is a form of intensive supervision or probation usually requiring an electronic device that is attached to the offender's body for tracking. These devices allow correctional staff to monitor offenders' movements and determine whether they have violated their restrictions.

> **❝** The offenders with whom electronic monitoring is commonly used include probationers, parolees, work releasees, pretrial releasees and others under community supervision. **❞**

According to [A.K.] Schmidt, there are two types of commonly used electronic monitoring devices: continuously signaling devices, which constantly monitor offenders at a particular location, and programmed contact devices, which provide periodic contact with offenders to verify their location. Both methods commonly require telephone use at the monitored location but can be operated using radio signals. [According to Schmidt,] with the continuously signaling method, the telephone "detects signals from the transmitter and reports to a central computer when it stops receiving the signal." Under the programmed contact method, [as M. Nellis states,] "a computer is programmed to call the offender during the hours being monitored either randomly or at specifically selected times." [Nellis continues,] when the computer calls the offender, "the wristlet is inserted into a verifier box connected to the telephone to verify that the call is being answered by the offender being monitored." Similarly, these methods can be replicated with radio transmitters monitored by either a mobile or a centralized receiver.

More recently, methods of electronically monitoring offenders have begun to use advanced cellular and global positioning satellite (GPS) technologies. Although the general process and practice remain the same, such technology allows for more consistent and precise tracking. As technology continues to expand, the potential options for monitoring offenders grow.

Electronic monitoring's origin

While the basic technology for electronic monitoring was developed by psychologist Robert Schwitzgebel at the University of California in the 1960s, the concept is cited to have been developed as early as 1919. [According to R. Enos et al.,] the idea's inception in the 1960s was proposed as an "adjunct to therapeutic work and as a means of reducing the prison population." In 1969, Schwitzgebel patterned a specific monitoring device. However, throughout the 1970s, little interest was shown in electronic monitoring as a sentencing alternative and the actual practice of electronically monitoring offenders did not begin until the 1980s. Inspired by the Spider-Man comic, New Mexico Judge Jack Love put electronic monitoring into practice in 1984.

Since its inception in 1984, the use of electronic monitoring as a correctional tool has grown rapidly. According to [P.] Elrod and [M.P.] Brown, electronic monitoring "has developed into one of the most popular community corrections sanctions in the United States." This popularity coincides with the larger "get tough" trend in corrections. According to [J.F.] Quinn and [J.E.] Holman, "the popularity of electronic monitoring is partially a result of the general trend toward a 'control orientation' in community corrections." According to a survey of citizen attitudes toward electronic monitoring, public support appears to be "strong, yet conditional." Public support is reported to be strong for using electronic monitoring on "minor" offenders but weak for "serious" offenders. Nevertheless, it is clear that as public opinion shifted to getting tough on crime in the 1980s and 1990s, electronic monitoring found a niche in corrections.

> *Outcome effectiveness concerns whether electronic monitoring provides an effective means of social control.*

According to Schmidt, the actual number of offenders being monitored is unknown. Nevertheless, one can obtain information concerning the use of electronic monitoring. [M.] Renzema reports that between 1986 and 1990, the number of electronically monitored offenders increased from 826 to 10,000. [K.E.] Courtright et al. report that this number "appears to be steadily increasing" and will likely continue to do so. In 1998, it was estimated that there were about 1,500 electronic monitoring programs and 95,000 units in use. And in England, by 2000, electronic monitoring or "tagging" (under the guise of "home detention curfews") had already been employed in more than 21,500 cases despite being first implemented in 1995. Considering the relative flexibility of electronic monitoring programs, it is difficult to obtain an accurate count of the actual number of offenders being monitored at any given time; nevertheless, studies such as those mentioned above have found that it is a popular alternative to incarceration.

> *Those sentenced to a combination of electronic monitoring and intensive drug therapy had lower recidivism rates than those who were not.*

The offenders with whom electronic monitoring is commonly used include probationers, parolees, work releasees, pretrial releasees and others under community supervision. According to [J.T.] Whitehead, "About one-third of the offenders were under electronic monitoring for property offenses, 22 percent for drug offenses, another one-fifth for major traffic offenses and approximately 12 percent for crimes against a person." Whitehead does not indicate whether driving under the influence (DUI) is included under "major traffic offenses," but Nellis reported that 26 percent of those electronically monitored were being sanctioned for drunken driving. As of a 1989 National Institute of Justice survey, approximately 90 percent of electronically monitored offenders were male. Additionally, 55 percent of electronically monitored offenders were younger than 30. As is true of the overall number of offenders, the variety of those who are electronically monitored is rapidly expanding. . . .

Outcome effectiveness

The use of electronic monitoring as an alternative to incarceration clearly evokes a variety of issues and concerns that should be addressed. Perhaps the greatest concern, however, is whether electronic monitoring is effective in its outcomes. Is it successful? Success may be defined in numerous ways depending on the particular jurisdiction or program. As previously indicated, the success of an electronic monitoring program may focus on savings or diversion, but what is meant by outcome effectiveness is something else: It generally refers to whether electronic monitoring is serving some of the more explicit functions of corrections—namely, whether it deters, incapacitates or punishes. In other words, outcome effectiveness concerns whether electronic monitoring provides an effective means of social control. . . .

Alternative to incarceration

Sometimes referred to as house arrest, electronic monitoring often is used as an alternative to institutional incarceration. In those cases, offenders are confined to their homes and monitored electronically to ensure that they are there at the required times. Some of the earliest research on electronic monitoring focused on such a situation. For example, in a qualitative assessment of the Community Control House Arrest Program in Florida, [J.E.] Papy and [R.] Nimer concluded that the program, as an alternative to incarceration, was "generally successful."

> *The offenders sentenced to probation committed more serious rule violations than those sentenced to electronic monitoring.*

In a study of a county home detention program in Indiana, [S.] Roy found that 86.8 percent of offenders successfully completed the program and of those 86.4 percent did not have a subsequent record of recidivism after one year. In a study focusing specifically on DUI offenders, Courtright et al. found that based on recidivism and technical violations, electronic monitoring was as effective as jail. Similarly, in a study focused on incarceration in a residential facility and work release program, [A.] Jolin and [B.] Stipak investigated whether any differences existed among three programs in Clackamas County, Ore. The first group of offenders had been sentenced to electronic monitoring without treatment opportunities. The second group had been sentenced to a work release program and were required to reside in a residential center. The third group consisted of convicted drug offenders who had been sentenced to electronic monitoring and were required to participate in intensive drug therapy. Results indicated that those sentenced to a combination of electronic monitoring and intensive drug therapy had lower recidivism rates than those who were not. Jolin and Stipak concluded that their research provided evidence that electronic monitoring, in conjunction with other treatment programs, can be an effective tool in preventing recidivism.

In a novel study of offenders' perceptions of electronic monitoring, [B.K.] Payne and [R.R.] Gainey found that, in general, offenders preferred electronic monitoring to incarceration but still viewed it as punitive. A follow-up study by the same authors found that some aspects of electronic monitoring were considered more punitive than incarceration. Their findings suggest that offenders experience difficulties similar to incarceration, as well as difficulties unique to electronic monitoring, including the cost the offender incurs, the negative impact on the offender's family relations, the stigma and embarrassment when out in public, and the discomfort from wearing the bracelet. . . .

Does electronic monitoring work?

[D.] Glaser and [R.] Watts conducted a study in Los Angeles in which the post-release records of 126 drug offenders sentenced to electronic monitoring were compared with 200 drug offenders who were sentenced to ordinary probation. They reported a statistically significant difference between the two groups: The offenders sentenced to probation committed more serious rule violations than those sentenced to electronic monitoring. In addition, those sentenced to standard probation had rule violations that largely consisted of "dirty" or missing drug tests, whereas the monitored group mainly violated curfew.

When electronically monitored offenders re-offended, they tended to commit more serious crimes.

Other studies have exhibited similar support for electronic monitoring as an additional element to community supervision. Quinn and Holman found that electronic monitoring contributed to stable levels of familial control, suggesting that the added element of electronic monitoring increased the external social control of offenders. [J.R.] Lilly, [R.A.] Ball, Curry and [G.D.] Smith found that 97 percent of electronically monitored probationers completed the electronic monitoring portion of the program and that 81 percent went on to successfully complete their probation. [L.A.] Gould and [W.G.] Archambeault found that offenders on "regular" probation were more likely to be rearrested. In addition, a recent study in England by [K.] Dodgson et al. found that offenders on an electronic monitoring "home detention curfew" program, as well as their families, reported significant advantages and success in the reintegration process following incarceration.

Not all findings regarding electronic monitoring are positive, however. For example, Dodgson et al. found no significant difference in reconviction rates between offenders released early on electronic monitoring and those serving their full sentence in prison. Gould and Archambeault found that electronically monitored offenders actually were more likely to be revoked for technical violations. [L.] Marye, [A.C.] Richards and [S.J.] Barthelemy, in a cross-sectional analysis of juvenile non-status offenders placed on electronically monitored home detention, also found a lack of support for outcome effectiveness for electronic monitoring. In fact, their findings suggest that the electronically monitored juveniles both violated program conditions and recidivated more often than the offenders who were placed in a community supervision program without electronic monitoring.

> *We have acquired the technology that at least gives us the option to more strictly control offenders in the community.*

Moreover, when electronically monitored offenders reoffended, they tended to commit more serious crimes. The study findings should be approached with some caution, however. Juveniles' participation in the electronic monitoring program was a voluntary alternative to incarceration; therefore, selection bias is inherent in the electronically monitored group such that they were likely to be higher-risk offenders than those in a community supervision program without electronic monitoring. Additionally, as was likely the case in the Gould and Archambeault study, if failure is measured by technical violations or revocation, there is inherent bias against those who are electronically monitored due to the increased supervision and likelihood of a violation being detected.

Research also indicates that, although a potentially successful community supervision tool, electronic monitoring is not a safe replacement for probation and parole officers. For example, Papy and Nimer, although finding electronic monitoring to be generally successful, assert that it should augment rather than replace officer supervision. Similarly, research by Beck et al. suggests that officer involvement in supervision remains critical to successfully supervise offenders in the community. . . .

The future of electronic monitoring

Ironically, the use of electronic monitoring began in 1984, a year that also is the title and setting of George Orwell's classic dystopian novel. Have we reached the era of Big Brother in which we can constantly monitor individuals? Has Orwell's tale come to fruition? Probably not; however, we have acquired the technology that at least gives us the option to more strictly control offenders in the community. That technology and its implementation continue to evolve rapidly and undoubtedly will expand. For example, electronic monitoring's use of GPS has evolved and increased immensely since it was first implemented in the late 1990s—from about 40 cases in 1998 to more than 635 as of mid-2000. However, as previously noted, the ever-evolving technology will no doubt create new levels of intrusiveness and will continue to be questioned regarding its ethical and constitutional feasibility.

While the use of increasingly advanced technology is clearly the future of electronic monitoring, a more important question is do we want electronic monitoring in the future of corrections? The offender population continues to grow, prison crowding has not subsided and money is always a concern. Is electronic monitoring an appropriate and realistic response to these concerns? It is difficult to say. The relatively sparse research provides no definitive answers, although, there is some support for its effectiveness. But the limited research has generally been plagued by a number of problems that severely undermine the findings. Where research is concerned, it can only be concluded that it is still unknown whether electronic monitoring is an effective alternative. What is known, however, is that the public supports it as an increased form of control over offenders in the community and that the increasing fear of crime by the public demands a "control orientation" in community corrections. For these reasons, the use of electronic monitoring is proliferating. Regardless of whether it saves money, or reduces recidivism or prison crowding, electronic monitoring will continue to evolve and is likely to remain a popular correctional alternative.

Organizations to Contact

The editors have compiled the following list of organizations concerned with the issues debated in this book. The descriptions are derived from materials provided by the organizations. All have publications or information available for interested readers. The list was compiled on the date of publication of the present volume; names, addresses, phone and fax numbers, and e-mail and Internet addresses may change. Be aware that many organizations may take several weeks or longer to respond to inquiries, so allow as much time as possible.

American Civil Liberties Union (ACLU)
National Prison Project
713 Fifteenth St. NW, Suite 620, Washington, DC 20005
(202) 393-4930 • fax: (202) 393-4931
e-mail: aclu@aclu.org • Web site: www.aclu.org

Formed in 1972, the ACLU's National Prison Project is a resource center that works to protect the Eighth Amendment rights of adult and juvenile offenders. It opposes electronic monitoring of offenders and the privatization of prisons. The project publishes the quarterly *National Prison Project Journal* and various booklets.

American Correctional Association (ACA)
4830 Forbes Blvd., Lanham, MD 20706-4322
(800) 222-5646 • (301) 918-1900
e-mail: jeffw@aca.org • Web site: www.aca.org

ACA is committed to improving national and international correctional policy and to promoting the professional development of those working in the field of corrections. It offers a variety of books and courses on the criminal justice system. ACA publishes the bimonthly magazine *Corrections Today*.

American Youth Policy Forum
1836 Jefferson Place NW, Washington, DC 20036
(202) 775-9731 • fax: (202) 775-9733
e-mail: aypf@aypf.org • Web site: www.aypf.org

The American Youth Policy Forum is a nonprofit, nonpartisan, professional development organization that provides learning experiences for national, state, and local policy makers and practitioners on youth issues. Its goal is to improve opportunities, services, and life prospects for youth. It offers a number of free publications online including *Less Hype, More Help: Reducing Juvenile Crime; What Works—and What Doesn't;* and *Less Cost, More Safety: Guiding Lights for Reform in Juvenile Justice.*

Cato Institute
1000 Massachusetts Ave. NW, Washington, DC 20001-5403
(202) 842-0200 • fax: (202) 842-3490
e-mail: cato@cato.org • Web site: www.cato.org

Cato is a libertarian research foundation working to limit the role of government and protect individual liberties. It contends that too many Americans are incarcerated because of the failing war on drugs. The institute has evaluated government criminal-justice policies and offered prison reform proposals in its publication *Policy Analysis*. In addition, Cato publishes the quarterly magazine *Regulation*, the bimonthly *Cato Policy Report*, and numerous books.

Center for Alternative Sentencing and Employment Services (CASES)
346 Broadway, 3rd Fl., New York, NY 10013
(212) 732-0076 • fax: (212) 571-0292
Web site: www.cases.org

CASES seeks to end what it views as the overuse of incarceration as a response to crime. It operates two alternative-sentencing programs in New York City: the Court Employment Project, which provides intensive supervision and services for felony offenders, and the Community Service Sentencing Project, which works with repeat misdemeanor offenders. The center advocates in court for such offenders' admission into its programs. CASES publishes various program brochures.

Critical Resistance
1904 Franklin St., Suite 504, Oakland, CA 94612
(510) 444-0484 • fax: (510) 444-2177
e-mail: ernational@criticalresistance.org
Web site: www.criticalresistance.org

Critical Resistance is an activist group opposed to caging and controlling people in prisons, maintaining that prison is not an effective response to poverty and crime. The group advocates the immediate release of all nonviolent offenders from the U.S. prison system. It publishes several reports offering alternatives to incarceration on its Web site, including *A Plan to Save the State of California a Billion Dollars*.

Families Against Mandatory Minimums (FAMM)
1612 K St. NW, Suite 700, Washington, DC 20006
(202) 822-6700 • fax: (202) 822-6704
e-mail: famm@famm.org • Web site: www.famm.org

FAMM is an educational organization that works to repeal mandatory minimum sentences. It provides legislators, the public, and the media with information on, and analyses of, mandatory-sentencing laws. FAMM publishes the quarterly newsletter *FAMMGram*.

Heritage Foundation
214 Massachusetts Ave. NE, Washington, DC 20002-4999
(202) 546-4400 • fax: (202) 546-8328
e-mail: pubs@heritage.org • Web site: www.heritage.org

The Heritage Foundation is a conservative think tank that advocates free enterprise and limited government. Heritage researchers support tougher sentencing policies and the construction of more prisons. Its publications include the quarterly *Policy Review* and online resources such as *Policy Research & Analysis*.

Justice Policy Institute
4455 Connecticut Ave. NW, Suite B-500, Washington, DC 20008
(202) 363-7847 • fax: (202) 363-8677
e-mail: info@justicepolicy.org • Web site: www.justicepolicy.org

The Justice Policy Institute is a nonprofit research and public policy organization dedicated to ending society's reliance on incarceration and promoting just and effective solutions to America's social problems. The Justice Policy Institute has published numerous reports and articles debating crime and punishment in America, including *Poor Prescription: The Cost of Imprisoning Drug Offenders in the United States* and *The Punishing Decade*.

Law Enforcement Alliance of America (LEAA)
7700 Leesburg Pike, Suite 421, Falls Church, VA 22043
(703) 847-2677 • fax: (703) 556-6485
e-mail: editor@leaa.org • Web site: www.leaa.org

Comprising more than sixty-five thousand members and supporters, the Law Enforcement Alliance of America is the nation's largest coalition of law enforcement professionals, victims of crime, and concerned citizens dedicated to making America safer. It publishes the quarterly journal the *Shield*.

National Center for Policy Analysis (NCPA)
601 Pennsylvania Ave. NW, Suite 900, Washington, DC 20004
(202) 628-6671 • fax: (202) 628-6474
e-mail: ncpa@ncpa.org • Web site: www.ncpa.org

NCPA is a public policy research institute that advocates more stringent prison sentences, the repeal of parole, and financial restitution for crimes. Publications include the periodicals *NCPA Policy Backgrounder* and *Brief Analysis*, which regularly address the issue of prisons. NCPA also publishes numerous papers and studies, including *Privatizing Probation and Parole* and *Crime and Punishment in America*.

National Center on Institutions and Alternatives (NCIA)
7222 Ambassador Rd., Baltimore, MD 21244
(410) 265-1490 • fax: (410) 597-9656
Web site: www.ncianet.org

NCIA is a criminal justice foundation that supports community-based alternatives to prison, contending that they are more effective at providing the education, training, and personal skills required for the rehabilitation of nonviolent offenders. The center advocates doubling "good conduct" credit for the early release of nonviolent first-time offenders in the federal prison system to make room for violent offenders. NCIA publishes books, reports, and the periodic newsletters *Criminal Defense Update* and *Jail Suicide/Mental Health Update*.

National Crime Prevention Council (NCPC)
1000 Connecticut Ave. NW, 13th Fl., Washington, DC 20036
(202) 466-6272 • fax: (202) 296-1356
e-mail: webmaster@ncpc.org • Web site: www.ncpc.org

NCPC provides training and technical assistance to groups and individuals interested in crime prevention. It advocates job training and recreation programs as a means to reduce crime and violence. The council, which sponsors the Take a Bite Out of Crime campaign, publishes the newsletter *Catalyst,* which comes out ten times a year.

National Mental Health Association
2001 N. Beauregard St., 12th Fl., Alexandria, Virginia 22311
(703) 684-7722 • fax: (703) 684-5968
Web site: www.nmha.org

The National Mental Health Association is America's oldest and largest nonprofit organization addressing all aspects of mental health and mental illness. Through advocacy, education, research, and service, NMHA works to improve the mental health of all Americans, especially the 54 million people with mental disorders, including many of those who are incarcerated. Its publications include many pamphlets, reports, and advocacy guides available free for downloading.

The Sentencing Project
514 Tenth St. NW, Suite 1000, Washington, DC 20004
(202) 628-0871 • fax: (202) 628-1091
e-mail: staff@sentencingproject.org
Web site: www.sentencingproject.org

The Sentencing Project seeks to provide public defenders and other public officials with information on establishing and improving alternative sentencing programs that provide convicted persons with positive and constructive options to incarceration. It promotes increased public understanding of the sentencing process and alternative sentencing programs. It publishes many reports on U.S. prisons including *Facts About Prison and Prisoners* and *Prison Privatization and the Use of Incarceration.*

Urban Institute (UI)
2100 M St. NW, Washington, DC 20037
(202) 833-7200
e-mail: paffairs@ui.urban.org • Web site: www.urban.org

UI is a nonpartisan research organization that conducts regular studies on a wide array of social issues. Its research on America's prison system maintains that inmates are not receiving enough rehabilitative programming or adequate life-skills preparation prior to release. Its reports on prison reform, posted on UI's Web site, include *A Portrait of Prisoner Reentry in Illinois* and *Parole in California, 1980–2000: Implications for Reform.*

U.S. Department of Justice
Federal Bureau of Prisons
320 First St. NW, Suite 501, Washington, DC 20004
Web site: www.bop.gov

The Federal Bureau of Prisons works to protect society by confining offenders in the controlled environments of prisons and community-based facilities. It believes in providing work and other self-improvement opportunities within these facilities to assist offenders in becoming law-abiding citizens. The bureau publishes the book *The State of the Bureau*.

Vera Institute of Justice
233 Broadway, 12th Fl., New York, NY 10279
(212) 334-1300 • fax: (212) 941-9407
e-mail: info@vera.org • Web site: www.vera.org

The Vera Institute is an activist group that works to ensure a fair and efficient criminal justice system for all Americans. The institute takes the position that the country has incarcerated too many nonviolent offenders who would be better served by drug treatment and educational programming. It publishes the monthly *Issues in Brief* and numerous reports on prison reform such as *Diverting Drug Abusers from Prison* and *Project Greenlight: Preparing Prisoners for Release*.

Volunteers of America
1660 Duke St., Alexandria, VA 22314
(703) 341-5000 • fax: (703) 341-7000
e-mail: info@voa.org • Web site: www.volunteersofamerica.org

Volunteers of America is a national, nonprofit, spiritually based organization providing local human service programs and opportunities for individual and community involvement. It provides outreach programs that deal with today's most pressing social needs, including helping at-risk youths, frail elderly, abused and neglected children, people with disabilities, homeless individuals, and many others. In addition to publishing reports and various press releases, it publishes the journal *Spirit* three times a year, as well as the *Gazette* six times a year.

Bibliography

Books

Thomas G. Blomberg and Stanley Cohen, eds.	*Punishment and Social Control.* New York: Aldine de Gruyter, 2003.
Ulla V. Bondeson	*Alternatives to Imprisonment: Intentions and Reality.* New Brunswick, NJ: Transaction, 2002.
Gail A. Caputo	*Intermediate Sanctions in Corrections.* Denton: University of North Texas Press, 2004.
Todd R. Clear and Harry R. Dammer	*The Offender in the Community.* Belmont, CA: Thomson/Wadsworth, 2003.
Angela Davis	*Are Prisons Obsolete?* New York: Seven Stories, 2003.
R.A. Duff	*Punishment, Communication, and Community.* New York: Oxford University Press, 2001.
Stephen Duguid	*Can Prisons Work? The Prisoner as Object and Subject in Modern Corrections.* Toronto: University of Toronto Press, 2000.
Joel Dyer	*The Perpetual Prisoner Machine: How America Profits from Crime.* Boulder, CO: Westview Press, 2000.
Joseph T. Hallinan	*Going Up the River: Travels in a Prison Nation.* New York: Random House, 2001.
Othello Harris, ed.	*Impacts of Incarceration on the African American Family.* New Brunswick, NJ: Transaction, 2003.
Tara Herivel and Paul Wright, eds.	*Prison Nation: The Warehousing of America's Poor.* New York: Routledge, 2003.
Peter G. Herman, ed.	*The American Prison System.* New York: H.W. Wilson, 2001.
Joy James, ed.	*States of Confinement: Policing, Detention, and Prisons.* New York: Palgrave, 2000.
Robert Johnson	*Hard Time: Understanding and Reforming the Prison.* Belmont, CA: Wadsworth, 2001.
Mark Jones	*Community Corrections.* Prospect Heights, IL: Waveland Press, 2004.
Ann Chih Lin	*Reform in the Making: The Implementation of Social Policy in Prison.* Princeton, NJ: Princeton University Press, 2002.

John P. May, ed.	*Building Violence: How America's Rush to Incarcerate Creates More Violence.* Thousand Oaks, CA: Sage, 2000.
Christian Parenti	*Lockdown America: Police and Prisons in the Age of Crisis.* New York: Verso, 2000.
Joan Petersilia	*When Prisoners Come Home: Parole and Prisoner Reentry.* New York: Oxford University Press, 2003.
W. Gordon West and Ruth Morris	*The Case for Penal Abolition.* Toronto: Canadian Scholars' Press, 2000.

Periodicals

Deborah Smith Bailey	"Alternatives to Incarceration," *Monitor on Psychology*, July/August 2003.
Phylis Skloot Bamberger	"Specialized Courts: Not a Cure-All," *Fordham Urban Law Journal*, March 2003.
Vince Beiser	"A Necessary Evil?" *Los Angeles Times*, October 19, 2003.
Etienne Benson	"Rehabilitate or Punish?" *Monitor on Psychology*, July/August 2003.
Paula Tully Bryant	"Florida's Award-Winning Nonsecure Drug Treatment Program," *Corrections Today*, June 2000.
Fox Butterfield	"Women Find a New Arena for Equality: Prison," *New York Times*, December 29, 2003.
Alan Elsner	"America's Prison Habit," *Washington Post*, January 24, 2004.
Julie Falk	"Fiscal Lockdown," *Dollars & Sense*, July/August 2003.
C. West Huddleston	"Jail-Based Treatment and Reentry Drug Courts," *American Jails*, March/April 2000.
Eli Lehrer	"Hell Behind Bars: The Crime That Dare Not Speak Its Name," *National Review*, February 5, 2001.
Los Angeles Times	"Roads to Rehabilitation," November 25, 2003.
Ed Marciniak	"Standing Room Only: What to Do About Prison Overcrowding," *Commonweal*, January 25, 2002.
Ayelish McGarvey	"Reform Done Right," *American Prospect*, December 2003.
Edwin Meese and Eric Holder	"Work for the Chain Gang," *Washington Times*, July 23, 2002.
George Miller	"A Smart Solution to Jail Crowding," *Corrections Today*, July 2000.
George Neumayr	"Crime and No Punishment," *American Spectator*, July 9, 2003.

Ernerst Partridge   "The Two Faces of Justice," *Free Inquiry*, Summer 2001.

Amanda Ripley   "Outside the Gates," *Time*, January 21, 2002.

Kit R. Roane   "Maximum Security Inc.," *U.S. News & World Report*, May 28, 2001.

Frank Rubino   "Doing Family Time," *Hope*, March/April 2004.

Margaret Talbot   "Catch and Release," *Atlantic Monthly*, January/February 2003.

Sanho Tree   "The War at Home," *Sojourners*, May/June 2003.

Richard D. Vogel   "Capitalism and Incarceration Revisited," *Monthly Review*, September 2003.

Kevin Warwick   "Intermediate Sanction Options Help Alleviate Jail Overcrowding," *American Jails*, November/December 2002.

Edward Wong   "Behind Bars and on the Clock," *New York Times*, June 6, 2001.

Katherine Van Wormer   "Restoring Justice," *USA Today Magazine*, November 2001.

Index